# WISING UP

Other Books by Jerry Minchinton

*MAXIMUM SELF-ESTEEM:*
*The Handbook for Reclaiming*
*Your Sense of Self-Worth*

*52 Things You Can Do to*
*Raise Your Self-Esteem*

**NOTICE:**

# WISING UP

## HOW TO STOP MAKING SUCH A **MESS** OF YOUR LIFE

JERRY MINCHINTON

ARNFORD HOUSE, PUBLISHERS
*A division of the arnford corporation*

Permissions
Arnford House, Publishers
Route 1, Box 27
Vanzant Missouri 65768.

---

Cataloging-in-Publication

Minchinton, Jerry.
    Wising up : how to stop making such a mess of
your life / Jerry Minchinton. – 1st ed.
    p. cm.
    ISBN: 0-9635719-5-8

    1. Interpersonal conflict. 2. Interpersonal
relations. 3. Conflict management.   I. Title.

BF637.I48M56 2000      158.2
             QB199-1299

---

Printed in the United States of America
10 9 8 7 6 5 4 3 2 1

# Contents


Acknowledgments   6

1 What's the Problem, Anyway?   10

2 Stan and Alec   20

3 Carla and Joan   36

4 Karen and Terri   52

5 Brian and Sally   70

6 Richard and His Father   88

7 Mikki and Paul   106

8 Melissa and Donna   122

9 Shana and Jason   142

10 Connie and the Solicitors   158

11 Joe and the Baseball Team   186

12 A Short Course in Solving Problems   209

Appendix: The Three Levels of Problem-Solving and   220

Profiles of Those Who Use Them

# Acknowledgments

This book is an outgrowth of two items: a personality profile created a few years ago by I and my business partner and friend, Clifford Bradley, and a chapter titled "Solving Problems," from an earlier book of mine, *Maximum Self-Esteem.*

I am profoundly grateful to Stacey Gilbert, Michael Gilbert, Jean Names, Suzanne Sutherland, Marilyn Minchinton, and Frank L. Martin III, who gave me the benefit of their unique insights, viewpoints, and collective wisdom. And although this is not an official Mensa publication, I am indebted to several Mensans who aided and abetted: Terry Minchinton, Elaine Johnson, and "The Comma Doctor," who generously gave me their thoughtful comments and suggestions. Special thanks also to Clif Bradley for permission to use material from the "Minchinton-Bradley Personality Profile," for his valuable suggestions and ideas, and for performing what must have seemed like endless proofreading. I owe all of these friends a debt of gratitude, not just for helping me improve this book, but for providing me with a cheering section on occasion.

I would also like to thank The Acorn Press for generously giving me permission to quote from Ramesh S. Balsekar's *Explorations Into the Eternal.*

Jerry Minchinton

A Tao Master one day read out for his monks a text not familiar
to them. When asked who the author was, he replied "If I tell
you that this text is of the Lord Buddha, you will venerate and
prostrate before it; if I tell you that this text is written by a
patriarch, you will ponder it with great respect though not with
the same veneration you would accord it if it were from the
Buddha himself; if I tell you it is written by an unknown monk,
you will not know what attitude to take; and if I tell you that
this text was written by our cook, you will laugh and mock at it."

RAMESH S. BALSEKAR

*Explorations Into the Eternal*

There are three levels from which we can respond to our problems:

> Level 1 approaches work only by accident
> Level 2 approaches work now and then
> Level 3 approaches almost *always* work.

And which of these Levels do we use most consistently? The two *least* successful ones! This book is about getting to Level 3.

CHAPTER 1

# What's The Problem, Anyway?

**W**hether by choice or necessity, most of us are social creatures, spending much of our time each day in the company of others. While our personal and professional relationships can be a source of great happiness and pleasure, they can just as easily be the origin of unpleasant feelings and distressing problems. What kind of problems? Extremely common ones, such as when you feel as though people

- are trying to run your life
- act unfriendly and hard to get along with
- try to blame you for things
- pick on you a lot
- seem unconcerned about your feelings
- behave rudely or unkindly to you
- expect too much of you
- fail to help you as much as you think they should
- pay too little attention to your needs.

Or when you
- feel misunderstood
- think your life is unhappier than most
- find it hard to say "no" when you know you should
- think you've been taken advantage of
- feel as though you've lost control of your life
- think life is unfair
- worry about others' opinions and whether they like you
- feel left out of things
- frequently feel let down by others.

Do many of these problems seem familiar? Most of us are well-acquainted with them.

## WHY WE FAIL TO SOLVE OUR PROBLEMS

We would all like to eliminate problems like these from our lives, but somehow, despite our best efforts and extensive experience, our problems seem to multiply rather than disappear.

What are we doing wrong? Why do we have so many problems? For many reasons, including some which may surprise you:

*We learn the wrong lessons from our mistakes.* For instance, someone caught lying may decide, not that lying is a bad idea, but that she must become more careful. A person who loses his temper in certain kinds of situations may incorrectly learn that it's better to entirely avoid those kinds of situations than it is to explore the reasons for his anger.

*We don't learn <u>any</u> lessons from our mistakes.* It has truly been said, "Those who do not learn from the past are condemned to repeat it." When we don't understand the part we play in creating our problems, we learn nothing from them. Consequently, when similar circumstances arise, we repeat our earlier mistake and recreate the problem. As millions of persons who have divorced and re-married can testify, lack of awareness often causes people to unconsciously recreate the very problems they are trying to escape.

*We continue to use strategies which don't work.* Even though a particular approach to a problem has failed repeatedly, we go on using it rather than considering new and possibly better approaches. Like Cinderella's step-sisters trying to force their feet into the tiny glass slipper, we think if we try hard enough and long enough we'll eventually make the problem fit our approach.

*We respond to problems with self-defeating behavior.* When we allow ourselves to react to difficulties with unpleasant emotions or with violent or destructive behavior, we seldom learn from them.

Although indulging in negative feelings may give us the satisfaction of a momentary release, it usually just creates additional problems.

***We've never learned _how_ to solve problems.*** Some of us were denied the opportunity to learn to solve problems because we had parents who discouraged us from thinking independently and making reasoned decisions. Others of us have patterned our problem-solving methods on those of questionable role models and, as a result, have learned ineffective responses which serve us poorly.

***We base our tactics on inaccurate or inadequate information.*** During our early years we all absorbed some faulty, biased, and incomplete data. Clearly, when we base our decisions on this erroneous information, they are almost certain to be wrong. Just as using the wrong ingredients spoils a recipe, wrong ideas lead to wrong conclusions.

***We try to solve the wrong problem.*** The only thing worse than using the wrong problem-solving techniques is trying to solve the wrong problem. Often, we fail to identify the actual problem confronting us and, instead, focus on matters that are either imaginary or are caused by the *real* problem. Since dealing with imaginary or unrelated issues doesn't eliminate the actual problem, it remains unsolved and we remain unhappy.

***We believe solving problems is somebody else's responsibility.*** We fail to acknowledge problems we've caused, because we either find it too painful to admit our errors (even to ourselves) or we lack the insight necessary to recognize them as our errors. Insisting we are guiltless, we deny accountability for unpleasant problems we've created and try to persuade others to fix them. Understandably, most people resist doing what is actually our work so nothing changes.

***We are rewarded for _not_ solving problems.*** Peculiar though it sounds, many people will reward us if we behave like victims. The value we perceive may not be apparent to others, but when we are unable to deal with a disaster of our own creating, we often receive and enjoy the sympathy, pity, encouragement, comforting hugs, and attention we get. In addition, if we specialize in always being on the losing end of things, our world seems more understandable, predictable, and (seemingly) more manageable.

Obviously, the "benefits" we receive for failing to solve problems are at best highly questionable.

## THE IMPORTANCE OF SOLVING PROBLEMS

Why is the ability to solve problems so critical? Because without it, you will be continually involved in stressful situations which make your day miserable and take away the joy of living.

Does this sound a little extreme or exaggerated? It isn't, because like ripples in a pool, your effectiveness in handling your problems radiates out to affect — for better or worse — some of the most important aspects of your life.

### Your Emotions

- *When you fail to solve problems,* you are inclined to beat yourself up emotionally. So not only do you have to put up with failure, you also have to deal with the negative emotions you generate in response to it, such as anxiety, disappointment, shame, guilt, anger, fear, and hate.

- *When you solve problems successfully,* unhappiness is rare and you feel comfortable and light-hearted most of the time.

- *A question to ask yourself:* Am I contented most of the time or am I frequently unhappy?

## Your outlook on life

- *When you typically choose ineffective responses,* the ongoing frustration you experience makes you habitually negative and encourages you to accept a pessimistic view of life.

- *When you usually react wisely,* you resolve difficulties effectively, your affairs run smoothly, and life seems pretty good to you.

- *A question to ask yourself:* Do I look forward to getting out of bed each day or do I dread it?

## Your self-confidence

- *When your problem-solving efforts fall short* you are likely to view yourself as bumbling, stupid, and ineffectual, which makes it easy to think of yourself as someone who *always* handles problems unsuccessfully.

- *When you resolve problems well,* you feel comfortable, secure, and capable of dealing with other complicated matters in the future.

- *A question to ask yourself:* Do I feel able to handle most of what comes my way each day, or do I often feel overwhelmed by problems?

## Your feelings about yourself

- *When you feel you generally handle matters poorly,* you feel bad about yourself, and the less successful you are, the worse you feel. Unless you feel good about yourself to begin with, failing to solve your problems can diminish your self-esteem.

- *When you can resolve problems with ease and avoid creating new problems,* you reinforce your good feelings about yourself and increase your self-esteem. If you make a mistake, your positive self-image makes it easier to take it in stride.

- *A question to ask yourself:* Am I comfortable with myself and my behavior at least ninety percent of the time?

As you can see, there are as many unpleasant consequences to *failing* to develop your problem-solving skills as there are beneficial results from cultivating them.

## WHAT THIS BOOK CAN DO FOR YOU

The techniques in this book can revolutionize your problem-solving abilities and bring you increased happiness and peace of mind. They do this by teaching you to

- *identify the actual problem.* Trying to improve matters by addressing non-problems is like trying to unlock your front door with your car key. To avoid this error and the frustration which accompanies it, you will learn about the three levels from which you can approach problems, making it easy for you to recognize the real issue.

- *discover your customary problem-solving style.* Our problem-solving efforts generally fall into one of three categories. As you read the scenarios that follow and select your answers, you will see a pattern emerge, indicating which category you choose most often. Once you've identified your dominant problem-solving style, you'll understand why it does or doesn't work, and if it doesn't, what you can do to fix it.

- *look at old problems in new ways.* When you experience the same problem again and again, it is because you haven't changed the way you look at it. When you gain greater insight into your problems, you can change your perspective and bring this destructive cycle to an end.

- *become aware of new options.* To improve your problem-solving skills, it is necessary for you to consider fresh possibilities and new ideas. By increasing your awareness of viable, alternative solutions, you multiply your chances of producing positive, pleasing results.

- *eliminate many problems permanently.* Although few of us realize it (and fewer still admit it), *we* cause many of our worst problems. When you discover how you unknowingly and needlessly frustrate yourself and others, you will recognize the warning signs and eliminate many problems before they start.

Clearly, these are important skills we all can use.

## HOW THIS BOOK IS ARRANGED

### The Scenarios

Following this chapter are ten scenarios, each of which outlines a familiar problem.

### The Answers

Immediately after each scenario you will find five or six possible responses. Choose the one you believe will best resolve the problem just described. If you find it difficult to pick just one answer, do this: first, eliminate the answer you find least appropriate; second, eliminate the *next* least appropriate, then continue eliminating the least appropriate answers until only one remains.

Because practical considerations limit space, you may find that none of the answers describes *exactly* what you would do. However, each of the three levels of problem-solving is represented at least once in every group of answers. Even if you do not find an ideal answer there, it is most likely that you'll choose an answer that uses the same approach.

If some solutions seem far-fetched or extreme, they seem so because you think differently than the people who would actually choose them. *All* the responses, however, from the very best to the absolute worst, are drawn from real life.

A suggestion: be honest with yourself! Some people will choose an answer not because it's what they would actually do, but because they think it will make them seem more admirable than they believe they actually are. In fact, trying to alter reality in this fashion will make it difficult for you to make any significant improvements in your life.

## The Explanations

After you've chosen the strategy you think will be most effective, you will discover:

- the Level from which you approached the problem
- if you've tried to solve the real problem, a secondary problem, or a non-problem
- the belief that prompted you to choose the answer you chose
- the results most likely to occur in response to your answer
- how the results of your choice will affect you emotionally
- how your choice will affect your feelings about yourself
- which approach to the problem *will* work.

Regardless of the level from which you've responded, make a point of reading about the answers from the other levels. This can give you new ideas for dealing with future problems and provide valuable insight into people's sometimes puzzling behavior.

## What's the Real Problem?

This section discusses the scenario and answers in greater depth, explaining why some approaches won't work and providing real-world solutions which will.

## Things to Do

This section has three sub-sections:

- *"Important Ideas to Consider,"* which is designed to make you aware of possibilities you may never have considered. These ideas can also be used as affirmations  if you find using affirmations helpful.

- *"Questions to Ask Yourself,"* which encourage you to examine the aspects of your life that relate to the current scenario.

- *"Experiments,"* which consists of practical, interesting applications that will help you develop your problem-solving skills and give you realistic ways to use your new ideas.

## DO I REALLY NEED THIS?

Will learning to solve your problems more effectively be worth the time it will take? You can answer this question yourself. Think of this: solving problems as you do now has brought you to where you are today. Is this where you want to be? If it isn't, read on.

## *Important Ideas to Consider*

- To live is to grow, and growth demands flexibility.
- The greatest deterrent to increased happiness is resistance to change.
- If you want things to be different for you, then you must become different.
- Acknowledging that you were wrong doesn't mean you're stupid, just wiser.

Onward!

# CHAPTER 2

# Stan and Alec

**S**tan feels frustrated. Alec has asked Stan to help him paint his house, and Stan would like to refuse. He has helped Alec with a number of other projects, and each time Alec promised to help him in return. But despite Stan giving him plenty of advance notice, Alec always finds a reason for not being able to return the favor. He usually says he has to work late or go out of town. There have even been a few times when Alec said he couldn't help because it was vitally important that he attend certain social engagements.

Stan knows Alec has been taking advantage of him, and while he'd like to say, "No" to Alec, there's a problem: Stan's wife, Angie, and Alec's wife, Paula, have been best friends ever since their high school days. Angie is afraid that Alec might get angry at Stan if he doesn't help him, and a rift between the two men would probably have a negative effect on her friendship with Paula. On previous occasions when Stan wanted to tell Alec he wouldn't help him, Angie always persuaded him that he should.

If you were in Stan's position would you . . .

**1** tell your wife you've hurt your back and won't be able to help Alec?

**2** try to convince a friend who owes you a big favor to do the painting for you?

**3** explain to both your wife and Alec that you are through providing free labor?

**4** help Alec because you know your wife's friendship with Paula is important to her?

**5** inform your wife you'll help Alec, but warn her this is the last time unless he returns the favor?

*If you chose*

**4** help Alec because you know your wife's friendship with Paula is important to her, or

**5** inform your wife you'll help Alec, but warn her this is the last time unless he returns the favor

*You think the problem is* keeping your wife from being unhappy.

*You think this is a problem because you believe* her happiness is more important than your own.

*You think it can best be solved by* helping Alec.

*PROBABLE OUTCOME:* You will do as Angie asks because you've resigned yourself to an ongoing, if reluctant, involvement with Alec and his projects. Although you may complain and threaten now, the next time he asks for your help, you'll allow yourself to be talked into helping him again.

Alec, of course, will call on you whenever he wants assistance in the future because he'll remember how cooperative (and inexpensive!) your help has always been.

*How is this likely to make you feel?* Angry, resentful, and victimized, because you correctly feel that others are taking advantage of you.

*Will you feel good about yourself?* No. Your self-respect shrinks whenever you allow yourself to be manipulated into doing something you'd rather not. No matter how you rationalize either of these answers consciously, on a deeper level you know you're selling yourself out. By compromising yourself in this fashion, you affirm, first, that your rights and wishes are less important than your wife's, and second, that you as a person are less important.

*For a better alternative* see the information about Answer 3.



*If you chose*

**1** tell your wife you've hurt your back and won't be able to help Alec, or

**2** try to convince a friend who owes you a big favor to do the painting for you

*You perceive the problem to be* having to help Alec paint.

*You think this is the problem because you believe* you should not have to help someone who doesn't help you in return.

*You believe it can best be solved by* gaining the cooperation of your wife or a friend.

*PROBABLE OUTCOME:* You may be able to avoid helping Alec this time, through either lying or persuasion. That is only postponing the inevitable, however, because Alec already thinks of you as an easy mark, and neither of these solutions is likely to cause him to change his opinion. If you expect to rely on made-up reasons to escape similar situations in the future, you'll have to learn to manufacture good excuses at a moment's notice, like Alec does.

*How is this likely to make you feel?* Pleased at first, and then angry and resentful. Initially, you'll be happy because you have avoided helping Alec — this time. But when he once again seeks your help, as he undoubtedly will, you'll experience the anger and resentment you only postponed with these responses to the problem.

*Will you feel good about yourself?* No. At first you'll praise yourself for being clever enough to have avoided the painting. But these good feelings will evaporate the next time Alec asks you for help, and you'll feel victimized, helpless, and inadequate when you realize you're no better off now than you were.

*For a better alternative* see the information about Answer 3.

### LEVEL 3 ANSWER

*If you chose*

**3** explain to both your wife and Alec that you are through providing free labor

*You perceive the problem to be* that you have let your wife manipulate you into being an unpaid servant.

*You think this is the problem* because you believe your wants, needs, and happiness are as important as hers.

*You believe it can best be solved by* refusing to be taken advantage of just to keep her happy.

**PROBABLE OUTCOME:** Alec will either have to persuade somebody else to help him or paint his house by himself. Angie may find it necessary to re-evaluate her friendship with Paula if she detects a layer of frost forming on their relationship. You, however, will enjoy more of the leisure time you work so hard to accumulate.

Since people we've allowed to use us object when we tell them no, Angie will probably become upset when you refuse to help Alec. If she does, she may withhold her approval in an attempt to manipulate you into changing your mind. If you have an unpleasant time of it, keep in mind that you shouldn't have to compromise your integrity and self-respect just to please your wife.

*How is this likely to make you feel?* Sympathetic, but happy. You are sympathetic because you know your wife will probably be unhappy with your decision. You, on the other hand, will be happy because you'll no longer be performing thankless tasks purely to please someone else.

*Will you feel good about yourself?* Yes, because you have affirmed that your wants and needs are as important as those of others, including your wife.

# What's The *Real* Problem?

Stan's problem wasn't *a)* finding an excuse to avoid helping Alec, *b)* getting someone else to paint for him, or *c)* that Alec never returned his favors. It was that in order to please his wife he had been allowing her to manipulate him into doing things that weren't even remotely his obligation.

Since Alec is the one who has benefitted materially from Stan's free labor, it may appear that he is the real villain of the piece. But in truth, it was Stan's wife, Angie who made his exploitation possible. If she hadn't coerced him into helping Alec, he would have refused the other man's requests long ago.

How did Stan solve this problem? *First,* by becoming aware that Angie had been manipulating him and, *second,* by realizing that his needs and desires were just as important as hers.

While he was reflecting on how easily he had been manipulated, he began to wonder about the future of a marriage in which one partner is expected to satisfy the unrealistic expectations of the other. As Stan now saw it, by requiring him to debase himself to keep her happy, Angie demonstrated her belief that Stan's happiness and self-respect were less important than her own, and indicated that she gave her friendship with Paula a higher priority than she gave her relationship with her husband. He wondered also if it might not be time to have a good talk about the matter or visit a marriage counselor.

Could Angie have handled the matter differently and still achieved her goal? Yes, because there was a much fairer alternative that would have allowed both her and Stan to retain their dignity and avoid manipulation. Rather than treating Stan as though he were a servant, she could have approached him as an equal and offered to do something *he* wanted her to do in exchange for his helping Alec. This kind of open negotiation would have increased their mutual trust and improved the quality of their relationship. Instead, Angie's attitude has had just the opposite effect.

Angie was able to convince Stan that the women's friendship would be at risk unless he could avoid angering Alec, and it is possible this is true. If it is, then Stan's refusal may mean the end of the relationship between the women. But if the tie between them is so fragile that it disintegrates because of an unrelated matter, then Angie and Paula's friendship is as one-sided as the arrangement between Alec and Stan.

# Manipulation

The term for the method Angie has been using to get Stan to do as she wished is called *manipulation.* In this context we can define it as "getting people to do what you want without giving them something they value in return."

How does manipulation work? When someone says to you, "If you don't help me clean my house I'm going to be mad at you," that person is attempting to manipulate you. He is not offering you anything except to withhold a display of bad temper, which he could do in any case. But if the same friend says, "If you'll help me clean my house, I'll take you to the baseball game this afternoon," and your friend knows you love baseball, that is not attempted manipulation because you are being offered something you value in exchange for your efforts.

Or if we tell someone, "I'll be very disappointed if you don't come to my party," we're trying to manipulate her by indicating she will be responsible for the state of our emotions, a highly dubious "privilege" at best. On the other hand, suppose we say, "If you come to my party, I'll introduce you to the famous producer you want to meet." If the person we're talking with is an aspiring actress and the famous producer actually *is* coming to the party, then we are non-manipulatively offering her something she desires in exchange for what we're requesting.

## WHY MANIPULATORS MANIPULATE

Why do people seek to manipulate us? For reasons ranging from the meanest to the most benevolent:

*They derive emotional satisfaction from others' negative reactions.* Some people, because they are so dissatisfied with themselves and their lives, try to create problems for us so we will feel bad, too. If they are able to make us unhappy or uncomfortable they can focus on our pain instead of their own and momentarily feel better.

*Manipulating others gives them a feeling of power.* People who consider themselves weak and believe they lack power sometimes try to manufacture it by persuading people to do as they wish. When they are successful, they experience a temporary feeling of domination. Unfortunately for them and those with whom they associate, the sensation dissipates quickly, and they must continually reinforce it.

*They believe they aren't important enough.* Some individuals believe they are so unimportant that others are unlikely to give them what they want simply for the asking. To make up for their lack of bargaining chips, they try to convince us we should feel guilty or ashamed if we do not do as they ask, thinking (often correctly) that our desire to avoid those painful feelings will be so great that we'll do what they want.

*They believe certain tasks are beneath them.* Some profoundly misguided people tend to regard us more as servants than as equals. Because of the lowly status they've assigned us, they expect us to do tasks they're averse to doing themselves, whether because of their ignorance, reluctance, laziness, or an unwillingness to clean up after themselves.

*They don't know how to do or get what they want.* Some people believe themselves incapable of achieving their goals directly, as mature adults do, so they feel they have no choice but to manipulate us so we will achieve their goals for them.

*They are sure their manipulation will benefit those manipulated.* This idea is embraced by fanatics of every kind, who have deluded themselves into believing they know what's best or right for practically everyone. Since they are certain they are gifted with a special insight, they feel gratified if they can manipulate "less knowledgeable" people like us into taking the path they've chosen.

In fact, most would-be manipulators are not genuinely bad; they are just weak, self-centered, insensitive, inconsiderate, and misguided. They think of those they seek to manipulate as members of a lower order of creature, a less important form of life, whose needs and desires are also less important. To manipulators, other people are less "real" than they are, somewhat like a clever puppy or a beast of burden, which is to say, a nice enough creature, but one without a real existence of its own.

## THE FORMS OF MANIPULATION

Manipulative techniques vary, but in general, manipulators try to get our emotions to work against us. They do this by saying or doing something they hope will induce in us guilt, shame, anger, fear, or some other uncomfortable emotion. They may imply, for instance, that our failure to do as they wish will bring about a major disaster. They may describe in minute detail the various kinds of unpleasantness that will occur if we neglect to take the action they suggest. They may insist certain things are our duty or responsibility, or they may appeal to us on the basis of morality, ethics, or anything else they think might persuade us to agree with them. Some will pull out every emotional stop and tell us of the horrible pain they'll experience if we "let them down." We may be told we'll feel better about ourselves, that we'll make the manipulator extremely happy, that he or she will love us forever, or any number of other essentially meaningless terms.

Manipulators' speech is frequently laced with phrases such as these:

"You should. . ."
"You ought to . . ."

"If I were you, I'd . . ."
"It's for the best,"
"I only want what's best for you,"
"You'll thank me for this later,"
"What will people say?"
"What will people think?"

They use these and many other phrases which imply we will suffer a censure or penalty of some kind if we don't meet the "obligation" they've chosen for us.

What element do all these techniques have in common? The manipulator offers us nothing we value in exchange for doing what he or she asks.

## THE "BENEFITS" OF MANIPULATION

Since manipulators often seem to get what they want, it appears as though manipulation works *for* them and *against* those being manipulated. But in fact, no one involved in manipulative transactions gains any real benefit. Appearances to the contrary, manipulation is a game played only by victims. Whether we manipulate or are manipulated, we lose. And interestingly, no matter which end of the manipulative spectrum we're on, we experience the same negative feelings, although not for the same reasons:

*Powerlessness*: Manipulators, because they feel powerless, try to create power for themselves by persuading others to do things for them. If we are manipulated we feel powerless, too, because we have allowed the manipulator to dictate our course of action.

*Inadequacy:* Manipulators believe they lack certain characteristics and skills possessed by most others, so they try to gain access to these qualities by "using" those they believe have them. If we are manipulated we feel inadequate, too, because we think if only we were smarter or quicker, we could have escaped or outwitted the manipulator.

*Victimization:* Manipulators feel victimized because they believe life has dealt unfairly with them and given them far less than they deserve. Those of us on the receiving end of their manipulation also feel victimized, because we feel we must do as the manipulator asks, even though we don't want to.

*Anger and frustration:* Manipulators often feel irritated and thwarted because those whom they try to manipulate either fail to do what they ask or do it differently than they wish. Those whom they manipulate experience the same feelings as they resentfully do what the manipulator wants them to do.

As you can see, when manipulation takes place *no one* wins. If we allow ourselves to be manipulated, we sacrifice our right to self-determination, our self-esteem, our time, money, or energy and, often, our principles. Letting others control us, however briefly, makes us undervalue and compromise ourselves.

If we manipulate others, we are diminished by our maneuvering. We surrender our self-respect, resourcefulness, and self-reliance when we try to use others to achieve our goals. Worse still, if we are successful, we remain childish, emotionally immature, and dependent throughout life.

## AVOIDING MANIPULATION

So what are we to do? Unless we have *knowingly* obligated ourselves, when we're asked to do something that *a)* we don't want to do, *b)* isn't our obligation, and *c)* isn't a genuine *need,* we can refuse with a clear conscience. We don't have to feel guilty. We don't have to get caught up in elaborate excuses or contrived explanations. When manipulators ask for our help, we just have to say, "No."

This will no doubt shock those who are accustomed to our acquiescence, and it will be difficult for us at first if we are in the habit of giving in to unreasonable people. But saying, "No," is an acquired ability, and we will discover that the more we use it, the more proficient we become.

It's fine to exchange favors with people, of course, and it is commendable to voluntarily help others who are literally unable to help themselves. But when people try to create a feeling of obligation in us or try to persuade us to do something we dislike just to please them, beware: no matter how much they emphasize that doing what they want will benefit us, it's rarely our welfare with which they're concerned.

## *Important Ideas to Consider*

- My time and energy are as valuable as those of anyone else.
- My "not wanting to" is at least as important as the other person's "wanting me to."
- I definitely do not have to do everything I am asked to do.
- I don't have to provide an excuse for not wanting to do something.
- Only people who want to manipulate me insist that I should.
- If I don't say "No," my silence can be taken as a "Yes."
- Cooperation is a good alternative to manipulation.
- It is easier to avoid being manipulated if I am not a manipulator myself.
- My wants, needs, and happiness are as important as anyone's.

- I have the right to say "No" to doing things I dislike or find objectionable or inconvenient.
- I am not stubborn or mean just because I don't want to do what others ask.

## Questions to Ask Yourself

- Do I often feel I've been taken advantage of?
- Do I attempt to manipulate others? If I do, what are my reasons?
- Do I think I would be able to avoid a lot of unpleasant tasks if I were smarter?
- Can people usually talk me into doing things I don't want to do? If they can, why do I let them?
- If I allow people to manipulate me, what manipulative approach seems to work best with me? What can I do to change this?
- Do I feel guilty when I don't do what people ask of me?
- Do I frequently feel uncomfortable, resentful, and angry? Do I feel that way more around some people than around others?

## An Experiment

When people attempt to manipulate you, tell them exactly how you feel about the matter in a positive, but firm manner. To prepare yourself for doing this, practice saying the phrases "No, thanks," "Thanks, I'd rather not," "Sorry, but I've made other plans," "No, I don't want to," "Because I don't want to," and "I don't have to give you a reason," until you can say them with sincerity and conviction. Your skill will improve quickly with experience.

# CHAPTER 3

# Carla and Joan

**W**hen Carla and Joan met through mutual friends, both were looking for a new place to live. Since they seemed to get along well, they decided to share an apartment.

Although they were alike in a number of respects, the women differed when it came to caring for their automobiles. Carla's job required her to use a car, so she made a point of keeping hers in good condition. Joan, on the other hand, was somewhat casual about steady employment and, as a result, didn't always have the money for car repairs.

All went well between the young women for several months until Joan's car broke down and she couldn't afford to repair it. Claiming she had some important business to tend to, Joan asked Carla if she could borrow her car. Although Carla was concerned about getting to work on time, she let Joan take the car after Joan promised to return it promptly.

A few hours later she was regretting her decision as she nervously waited for Joan to return. Finally, just minutes before she had to leave for work, Carla called a co-worker and asked for a ride. Upon arriving at work, she had to borrow her supervisor's car. When she got home after work, she found an extremely apologetic Joan waiting. She'd been delayed, she said, because she'd gotten a flat tire and had to have it repaired.

On Wednesday, Joan once again appealed to Carla to use her automobile, saying she had an important interview for a well-paying job. Although Carla was hesitant because of what happened the last time Joan used it, Carla finally agreed, only to have to call a friend to take her to work when once again Joan didn't return in time. Carla's supervisor was less understanding this time and gave Carla a written warning for failing to bring an automobile for work. Then the supervisor notified Carla that if she showed up again without a car, she was likely to lose her job.

On Friday, Joan received a phone call that seemed to disturb her. As soon as she hung up, she hurriedly explained to Carla that it was vitally important that she borrow her car because her brother had been badly injured in an accident, and she had to go to the hospital to see him. Although Carla was still irritated because of Joan's previous failures to return her car on time, the situation seemed pretty serious.

If you were Carla, would you . . .

**1** discuss the situation with Joan, to see if you can work out something?

**2** tell Joan you're sorry but you can't lend her your car again?

**3** alert a friend who lives nearby that you might need to borrow her car?

**4** understand that Joan is having problems and give her another chance?

**5** tell Joan you'll take her where she wants to go before you go to your job and pick her up after work?

*If you chose*

**3** alert a friend who lives nearby that you might need to borrow her car, or

**4** understand that Joan is having problems and give her another chance

*You perceive the problem to be* making sure that Joan has transportation.

*You think this is a problem because you believe* you should help those who have problems.

*You believe it can best be solved by* lending your car to Joan again.

*PROBABLE OUTCOME:* You will lend your car to Joan and, since she's unlikely to return it on time, you'll have to borrow someone's automobile or get fired. Sooner or later even the dimmest of your friends will realize your lack of transportation is your problem, not theirs, and refuse to lend you their cars. And no matter how kind your supervisor or how convincing your story, if you arrive at work without your car again, she will fire you because she knows that you determine who uses your automobile.

*How is this likely to make you feel?* Resentful, angry, and concerned. If you chose either of these responses, you may as well give Joan your checkbook, credit cards, and pocket change, too, because in helping her escape the effects of her actions, you have taken them on yourself. If you lose your job, which seems quite likely, you will be concerned about being jobless and angry with both yourself and Joan.

*Will you feel good about yourself?* No. Even though you have made yourself a victim, you feel victimized by Joan, and possibly by your friends and supervisor, because of their reluctance to share the burden you've unnecessarily accepted. Unless you begin looking out for yourself, you will often find yourself in the same kind of situation in the future, since people will take advantage of you because it is so easy. You may eventually reach a point where you believe you deserve this treatment, which is the death knell of a major portion of your self-esteem. And if this isn't bad enough, because you feel forced to rely on others for transportation and sympathy, you will also feel inadequate and dependent.

*For a better alternative* see the information about Answer 2.

## LEVEL 2 ANSWERS

*If you chose*

**1** discuss the situation with Joan, to see if you can work out something, or

**5** tell Joan you'll take her where she wants to go before you go to your job and pick her up after work

*You perceive the problem to be* keeping Joan from being unhappy with you.

*You think this is a problem because you believe* it's important that people like you.

*You believe it can best be solved by* working out a compromise with Joan.

*PROBABLE OUTCOME:* By being so accommodating you remove Joan's incentive to repair her own vehicle. After all, why should she go to the bother when you're willing to be her unpaid chauffeur and/or allow her to avoid those distressing bills for gas, insurance, and repairs? Considering the extra expense and inconvenience you'll have, you will end up paying quite a high price merely to use your own car. To compound the problem, you'll still have to face Joan's disapproval when finally, in desperation, you rebel and let her know your feelings.

*How is this likely to make you feel?* Pleased, then irritated, frustrated, and angry. Initially, you will be pleased with yourself for being able to help Joan and also keep your job. But having come to her aid so often, you (and probably Joan, too) will feel you're obligated to continue helping her. Consequently, you will regret your generosity when you grow tired of driving for two and find that Joan depends on you.

*Will you feel good about yourself?* No. As a result of your good intentions you'll feel weak, inadequate, and powerless. Adding insult to injury, you'll lower your opinion of yourself because you made it so easy for Joan to take advantage of you.

*For a better alternative* see the information about Answer 2.

*If you chose*

**2** tell Joan you're sorry but you can't lend her your car again

*You perceive the problem to be* putting your job in jeopardy by being unwisely generous to Joan.

*You think this is a problem because you believe* your own needs must come first in your life.

*You believe it can best be solved by* letting Joan handle her own transportation problem.

*PROBABLE OUTCOME:* You will keep your job and Joan will be forced to find another solution to her problem. If she becomes upset when you refuse her, she may decide she no longer wants to share the apartment with you. Bearing in mind her lack of consideration and ready cash, that would probably be a great stroke of luck for you. It is true that you would have the inconvenience of finding another roommate, but if you're more selective, you'll find one who is both responsible and financially stable.

*How will this make you feel?* Sympathetic, but happy. While Joan's plight may elicit your sympathy, you realize that your first responsibility is to yourself, which means keeping your car so you can keep your job. You also realize that by helping Joan further, you not only encourage her to ask for additional favors, you also remove any reason for her to help herself.

*Will you feel good about yourself?* Yes. You've done what you know is best for you and for the other person.

# What's the *Real* Problem?

At the beginning of this scenario, it is *Joan* who has the problem. Carla, however, quickly develops a problem of her own by agreeing to help Joan solve *her* problem. After twice lending Joan her automobile and having it returned late, Carla is once again trying to decide whether she should continue solving Joan's problem, which may appear to be a lack of transportation but is, in fact, an aversion to steady employment coupled with a desire to escape responsibility.

If, despite Joan's previous failures to return her car on time, Carla chooses a Level 1 answer, it could be for a number of reasons, none of which are justified. She may mistakenly believe she has an obligation to always help others, no matter how much inconvenience it causes her. She might be afraid Joan will become angry or move out if she refuses. Granted, it wouldn't be pleasant sharing an apartment with someone who was angry with you and it would be inconvenient to have to find another person to help with the rent, but which would be worse — those alternatives or losing her job and possibly her apartment?

While it would be generous of Carla to play chauffeur or be willing to work out other arrangements as she does in the Level 2 answers, in the long run it is in the best interest of both of them for Joan to develop her own solutions. Of course compassion and understanding are important elements in all relationships, but when people can solve their own problems and we do it for them, we do them a great disservice.

When Carla chose the Level 3 solution, it was because she finally realized two important facts: *first,* that she is not obligated to solve others' problems when they can solve them themselves, and *second,* that she has given Joan no incentive to fix her own car. Only when having her own transportation becomes important enough to Joan will she go back to work to earn at least enough money to fix her car.

But what if Joan's brother is dying or his injuries are life-threatening? This would be tragic, of course, but if this were the case Joan might tie up Carla's car for days. While Carla may seem lacking in kindness in refusing to let Joan borrow her car again, her refusal doesn't prevent Joan from exercising other options. She could, for instance, use another friend's car, call for a taxi, take a bus, hitchhike, or, as many people do, walk.

While it may appear as though Carla is the only victim in this story, she is not. Her misguided help also caused inconvenience and additional expense to those who gave her a ride or loaned her a car. In helping Joan escape the consequences of her actions, Carla unwisely took them on herself, and then, just as Joan had done, tried to get others to help her avoid the consequences of *her* actions.

As far as Joan's failure to return Carla's automobile on time, two possibilities seem most likely: *1)* Joan's excuses were legitimate, and she *did* intend to return the car on time but was prevented from doing so by unexpected circumstances, or *2)* her excuses were fabrications made up to disguise a lack of responsibility. But the truth or falsity of Joan's stories isn't the issue. What *is* important is that Carla finally realized that letting Joan or *anyone* use her car under similar circumstances may cause some serious difficulties for her. Concern for others' problems can be admirable, Carla finally concluded, but not at the cost of her personal well-being.

# Helping Out

Although most of us don't mind doing favors now and then, hardly anyone wants to make a career of it. Unhappily, some people have no qualms about inconveniencing others if doing so helps them achieve their goals. People like this need no encouragement to try to make us their personal servants. Once they've zeroed in on us, we may be asked to do almost anything: provide transportation, repair plumbing, groom a dog, run errands, make a loan, or perform thousands of other unwelcome activities. When we have exhausted our largely ineffective stock of delaying tactics and feel we have no choice but to give in to their requests, we do it sullenly, resenting those we feel unable to refuse and despising ourselves for our weakness. Although helping these people may give us some pleasure initially, our good feelings vanish when we finally realize we are being used.

## WHAT TO DO WHEN PEOPLE ASK TOO MUCH OF US

Just what are our obligations when others seek our help? Obviously, there is no "one-size-fits-all" answer. While it would be unwise to thoughtlessly agree to do whatever others ask, it would be unkind and unfeeling to automatically refuse their requests.

What shall we do then, the next time we're asked for a favor and are uncertain whether to grant it? Here are some guidelines to make our decisions much easier:

*Assess the relative importance of what you're asked to do.* While some people ask for assistance only when matters are serious, others have no qualms about wasting our time on trivia. It is simpler, therefore, to learn to categorize another's request for help as either a *need* or a *want.* Once we've made this distinction, we may agree to drive across town to pick up someone's medication, but we won't play chauffeur for someone searching for a lampshade in exactly the right shade of pink. When we are clear on the differences between needs and wants, we are less likely to let others' persuasiveness triumph over our common sense.

*Put your own needs first.* Those who told us it was selfish to put our personal welfare before others' may have believed they were giving us sound advice, but unless they were trying to prepare us for sainthood, they were not. Although self-sacrifice sounds noble, it is impractical and potentially disastrous. Since we can't rely on others to look out for us, we must do it ourselves, which means making our personal requirements our highest priority. Only when we can adequately provide for our own needs will we be in a position to help those who can't. It is good to remember that although we may not be the most important person in the world, we are the most important person in *our* world.

**Don't help people who are able to help themselves.** There is an ocean of difference between those who genuinely require help and those who could handle matters themselves but prefer not to. When we help people who don't need it, we encourage their dependency and let them believe they can avoid responsibility for their lives.

Although we may face objections when we refuse to help the able, in the long run everyone comes out ahead when people learn to take care of themselves. Keep in mind that sometimes *not* helping people is a greater favor than coming to their aid.

**Stop being nice when you don't feel like it.** We are not obligated to do things for people merely because they ask us. If we are asked to do something we'd rather not, we are free to say no. Not only will this increase our self-respect, it will increase others' respect for us. When we have trouble refusing, we are easily victimized and are often looked on with contempt. If we do not say "Yes" every time we

are asked, people will be more appreciative of our help when we give
it.

*Pay no attention to your popularity rating.* Some of us are afraid
to be firm or assertive because we think others will dislike us or
become angry, and, of course, it is possible they will. But those who
resent our standing up for ourselves aren't the kind of people who
will be our friends, anyway. They are only interested in our welfare
to the extent that it affects their own. Trying to please others won't
make us well-liked — just overworked and under-appreciated.

*Don't solve problems people have created for themselves.* When
someone's life seems to consist of a series of disasters, it's often
because he creates problems for himself through lack of planning or
lack of concern for consequences. Unfortunately, people who are in
the habit of creating problems rarely want our advice, just our
assistance. Helping those with self-created problems is usually a
waste of time and effort because unless people are allowed to
experience the effects of their actions, they have little reason to
change them.

*Don't help people who can help you in return, but don't.* If past
favors remain unreturned, we have no obligation to perform any
more. One-way streets are for traffic, not human relationships. And
don't naively assume that sooner or later the person asking will
guiltily realize he's already asked too much and apologetically cease
his requests. Chances that this optimistic scenario will ever take place
are more than a million to one. Those who continually ask favors of
us and fail to repay them don't think of us as a fellow human being
but as a somewhat useful object, like an umbrella or a toaster.

*Treat your family members like people.* Some of us have been afflicted with relatives who believe that their kinship entitles them to behave inconsiderately and unreasonably. Respond to them as you would to any non-family member. Close relationships should be a source of love and happiness, not an excuse for exploitation. It is helpful to remind ourselves that family members are human beings first and relatives second, and we should judge their requests on their merits, not their location on the family tree. It is true blood is thicker than water, but it's also considerably more expensive.

*Avoid compromising your ethics or principles.* At one time or another most of us have been asked to lie or falsify information for another person and have felt uncomfortable at the idea of doing it. This kind of request puts us in an awkward position; we don't want to anger the person making it, but neither do we want to do something that is contrary to our principles. Be clear about this: *no one has the right to ask us to compromise our ideals, values, conscience, or reputation.* Those who do are thinking only of themselves.

*Set a realistic limit to your giving.* "Give till it hurts" is poor advice, whether it pertains to our time, money, or energy. If we deprive ourselves of necessities in order to give to others, we are likely to become resentful toward those we help when we realize our gifts are prompted by guilt rather than generosity. A better and more realistic motto would be, "Give as long as you enjoy it, and stop when it causes you pain." If we establish limits *before* a favor is asked of us, we will be in a much better position to say "No" when we should.

Essentially, there are three things we can do to protect ourselves from unreasonable requests. *First,* become familiar with the ideas listed above.

*Second*, learn to apply them to requests others make of us (and maybe even to requests *we* make of others). By taking these two steps, we will acquire the mental clarity needed to eliminate many irritating and inconvenient activities from our lives and gain the courage to refuse unreasonable demands. *Third*, we must learn to appreciate our value as a human being and increase our self-esteem and self-respect. When we are conscious of our true worth, we will automatically be a staunch advocate for our own rights.

While it is great to be able to give help to others when they genuinely need it, where do we draw the line? Does being compassionate mean we must bend over backward when others ask us to or that we must assist in solving everyone's problems or gratifying their desires? Definitely not. When helping others causes problems for us, it is time for a careful review of ourselves and our objectives.

Life is infinitely more pleasant when we possess the ability to comfortably refuse unreasonable or inconvenient requests. If we'd like to refuse obligations that aren't really ours and want to avoid feeling angry and resentful when people don't respect our needs, we must keep one important fact in mind:

> *If we don't acknowledge and respect ourselves*
> *and our needs, neither will anyone else.*

## *Important Ideas to Consider*

- It's up to me to look out for my own interests.
- My first obligation is to myself and my well-being.
- Sometimes I may do people a favor by not doing as they ask.
- My needs and requirements deserve the highest priority.
- Other people are probably thinking about what is best for them, not best for me.

## *Questions To Ask Yourself*

- If I don't look out for myself, who *will* look out for me?
- Is my attitude toward helping others realistic?
- Do I help others when it would be better for them to operate on their own?
- Do I ask people for help when I don't actually need it?
- Do I often feel resentful because I let people talk me into doing things I dislike?
- Do I knowingly allow people to take advantage of me because I don't know how to refuse?
- Do I ever let fear of someone's anger or dislike persuade me to do as they ask, even when I know I shouldn't?

## *Experiments*

1) Practice saying "No." Say it aloud, say it in your mind, and say it to yourself in the mirror. Mentally recreate past situations where you should have said *no* but didn't, and imagine repeating the situation, but firmly and finally saying *no*. Remember that, in declining to do things you don't want to do, you're being truthful and honest and increasing your self-respect.

2) Make a list of five or six phrases that are polite but nonetheless clearly and truthfully state that you decline to do what is being asked of you. Say these phrases over and over each day until you feel thoroughly comfortable saying them. Begin with something such as, "I'm afraid I've made other plans," or "I'm sorry, but it won't be convenient to do that."

3) Establish your personal standards for essential and non-essential requests. (It may be a good idea to put this list on paper so you can review it at intervals, if necessary.) Here are some questions that can help you make up your mind.

- Is the situation an actual emergency?
- Would the one asking me be willing to repay me in some manner if he or she were able?
- Will helping cost me money or time I can't afford to spend?
- Is my assistance being asked for a "need" or a "want?"
- Am I being asked to do something those asking can do themselves?
- Will helping be an inconvenience for me?
- Is it something I genuinely dislike doing?
- Am I being asked to help someone solve a self-created problem?
- Will doing what I'm being asked to do violate any of my personal rules for living?

# CHAPTER 4

# Karen and Terri

**D**isliking the impersonal atmosphere of the large university she was attending, Karen decided to transfer to a smaller college in Massachusetts. Once there, she found the new school to be much as she had hoped. With fewer students and smaller classes, it was easy to get to know people and she had already made a number of good friends since her move.

One Friday afternoon, when she discovered her last class of the day had been canceled, Karen decided to use her extra time to begin reading the new novel her mother had just sent her. To make the situation even more pleasurable, she went to the Italian restaurant next to her apartment house so she could enjoy some of their excellent espresso while she read.

A few minutes later she was seated in the restaurant's back booth, contentedly sipping coffee and enjoying her book. So engrossed was she in the story that at first she wasn't aware anyone had been seated in the booth behind her until she heard some young women begin chatting. At first she thought their talk might be distracting, but the novel was so compelling she found it easy to ignore their conversation, until, that is, someone mentioned her name.

The women began talking about her appearance. They made fun of her clothing, made nasty remarks about the way she wore her hair, and went on to add unkind comments about her makeup. Because of the way the booths were designed, Karen couldn't see any of the people sitting behind her, but as she listened, she was able to identify two of the voices. One belonged to Terri, who had been pointed out to Karen as the most popular girl on campus, and the other to Terri's friend, Arlene, whose braying laugh was unmistakable.

As the women continued talking, an unpleasant mixture of emotions washed over Karen. Why, she wondered, had these people she barely knew singled her out for this unkindness?

If you were Karen, would you . . .

**1** decide Terri and her friends probably spent a lot of time trying to impress people?

**2** stand up and tell Terri and her friends exactly what you think of them?

**3** find out where Terri shops and buy your clothing there from now on?

**4** wish they'd hurry up and leave so you could concentrate on your book?

**5** sit there quietly until Terri and her friends left, hoping they wouldn't see you?

**6** call a close friend and ask her opinion of your appearance?

*If you chose*

**2** stand up and tell Terri and her friends exactly what you think of them, or

**5** sit there quietly until Terri and her friends left, hoping they wouldn't see you

***You perceive the problem to be*** that people are making fun of you.

***You think this is a problem because you believe*** you do not compare favorably with others.

***You believe it can best be solved by*** avoiding people like Terri and her friends, or by making them want to avoid *you.*

*PROBABLE OUTCOME:* You will try to avoid Terri and her friends, hoping that staying out of their way will allow you to escape their future attention. But these tactics will neither affect your appearance or solve the actual problem, which has little to do with how you look. While Answer 2 may embarrass Terri and her friends briefly, it will probably just encourage them to be more careful where they indulge their passion for gossip and rancor. Answer 5, although largely ineffective, may save you from the greater humiliation of having to confront the women face-to-face. A major disadvantage of these "solutions" is that trying to avoid anyone who might be critical of you will require you to will lead a highly restricted life.

***How is this likely to make you feel?*** Hurt, embarrassed, despondent, rejected, and possibly angry or hateful. By choosing either solution, you indicate that you believe the women's unflattering comments are, for the most part true, and that your appearance (and probably you, yourself) are inferior. Although you agree with much of what they said, you resent them for verbalizing the self-defeating thoughts and feelings you try to ignore.

***Will you feel good about yourself?*** No. Because you believe unattractiveness has been unfairly inflicted on you, you feel not only inadequate, but victimized. Rather than reacting to the women's remarks with the determination to change your appearance, you respond with hopeless resignation, further diminishing your self-respect.

***For better alternatives*** see the information about Answers 1 and 4.

## LEVEL 2 ANSWERS

*If you chose*

**3** find out where Terri shops and buy your clothing there from now on, or

**6** call a close friend and ask her opinion of your appearance

***You perceive the problem to be*** that you are not as well-groomed and well-dressed as Terri and her friends.

***You think this is a problem because you believe*** other persons are better judges of your appearance than you are.

***You believe it can best be solved by*** relying on others' ideas and opinions to guide you in improving your appearance.

***PROBABLE OUTCOME:*** You will try to change your appearance by altering your makeup, hairstyle, and type of clothing in order to gain the approval of people like Terri. If you succeed at your goal, you may gain some self-assurance from resembling the "in crowd," but you won't be any happier, because all you'll have changed is the *outside* of yourself, when the part that is troubling you is on the *inside*.

*How will this make you feel?* Hopeful, disappointed, unhappy, uncomfortable, and dissatisfied. You will continue to feel discontented because your unhappiness isn't due to how you look, but to how you feel about yourself. Unless you change your feelings about yourself, you will continue to feel dissatisfied.

*Will you feel good about yourself?* No. By comparing yourself with others in this manner, you make yourself feel inadequate, ill-informed, and inferior. Plus, by becoming a copy of other persons, you sacrifice some of your individuality and integrity.

*For better alternatives* see the information about Answers 1 and 4.



*If you chose*

**1** decide Terri and her friends probably spent a lot of time trying to impress people, or

**4** wish they would hurry up and leave so you could concentrate on your book?

*You perceive the problem to be* the insecurity of Terri and her friends.

*You think this is a problem because you believe* they would not make unflattering comments about others if they were comfortable with themselves.

*You believe it can best be solved by* the young women, themselves.

*PROBABLE OUTCOME:* Terri and company will either move on to a more interesting subject or go on entertaining themselves at others' expense. Once you stop being their main topic of conversation, you will go back to enjoying your book, not, however, without making a mental note that striking up an acquaintance with any of Terri's group would not be worth your time and effort.

*How will this make you feel?* Possibly irritated at first, but then amused, entertained, and sympathetic. Initially, you may feel indignant or even angry. But then, realizing that people who make unkind comments about others usually do so because they feel insecure and inferior, you understand the problem isn't with you or your appearance, but with the women.

*Will you feel good about yourself?* Yes. Believing you are the best judge of your appearance, you have avoided creating a problem for yourself by refusing to become concerned with the remarks of Terri and her friends.

# What's the *Real* Problem?

The problem is not whether Karen needs to change her appearance, but whether she should attach any importance to the women's unkind comments.

If she chooses a Level 1 answer, it is because she believes the young women's criticisms are valid. Whether she responds actively, by telling the women what she thinks of them, or passively, by trying to avoid them, she feels it is futile to try to improve her appearance  because there is little or nothing she can do.

If Karen selects a Level 2 response, it is because she has accepted Terri and her friends' unkind remarks at face value, but rather than accept them passively, she resolves to modify her appearance to more closely match that of Terri and her friends, hoping to silence her critics by becoming more like them.

Although this strategy may keep this group from ridiculing her in the future, it has serious shortcomings. If she *is* able to copy Terri's personal style successfully, what should she do if two weeks later she hears *different* people criticizing her because she doesn't look more like *them*? Should she change again to please her new critics? And if she does, how many more times will she do it before she finally says, "Enough is enough," and dresses to please herself, which is what she should have been doing to begin with?

Fashion, someone has said, is a matter of who can conform the fastest. Karen has attracted the attention of Terri and her friends because, unlike them, she *hasn't* conformed. Her detractors' remarks don't indicate there's anything actually wrong with her, only that they are dissatisfied with her because she doesn't look more like them. If she thinks about it, Karen will realize the women's comments, despite their unkindness, are actually a compliment to her independence.

That is why the Level 3 answers will work best. If Karen has plenty of internal approval, she'll mentally grant Terri and her group the right to think anything they choose about her. Realizing that people's opinions are, for the most part, unimportant, she'll place little or no value on the remarks from the booth behind her. Understanding their comments are merely their personal opinions, she'll go on making decisions about her appearance based on what *she* thinks is best, instead of what others are wearing.

# Individuality and Conformity

We imitate others in more ways than we can imagine, including how we dress ("This style is very popular this year,"), what we think ("Everybody knows that!"), the books we read ("You have to read it! It's on the best-seller list"), the schools we attend ("The *best* people go to Harvard,"), and even the religion we adopt ("Our family has *always* attended this church").

We follow traditions carefully, not because we have necessarily determined their viability through our own experience, but because *most* people follow them. We live as we do not because we've found it is wise but because it's how *most* people live. We believe certain ideas are true not because we've seen evidence that they are, but because *most* people believe they are. We carefully perform some actions and just as carefully avoid performing others, not because we've investigated and found it was sensible to do so but because it's what everyone else seems to do.

Influenced by advertising, peer pressure, and authority figures, we have absorbed others' ideas about what we should think and say and how we should behave. Rather than defining our values for ourselves through careful study, we have accepted others' ethics and principles. Instead of selecting religious beliefs because they seem wise, reasonable, and humane, we have acquired our spirituality off the rack, so to speak, and subscribe to doctrines and dogmas others have created.

**WHY WE CONFORM**

There are sometimes practical reasons for our conformity, such as legal penalties we may incur if we are too different. The real impetus behind our slavish imitation, however, is the weight of social pressure. From the crib to the cemetery plot, whether at home, school or work, we are encouraged to imitate others' behavior by almost everyone with whom we come in contact. And generally, since there are so many people who expect us to conform, we find it easy to give in, convincing ourselves it's the best thing to do.

If we are courageous enough to protest that we don't *want* to do what most people do, we are presented with an abundance of ill-considered reasons why we should. Generally, these describe in vivid detail the extreme shock or horror people would supposedly experience if we behaved contrary to their expectations. Others try to deter us by predicting the distressing, possibly disastrous consequences we're likely to experience if we fail to rein in any individualistic tendencies. Here are some extremely familiar phrases:

- "You don't want to attract attention by being different, do you?"
- "What will people think of you?"
- "Don't you want to fit in?"
- "What would happen if *everybody* did what you want to do?"
- "Why can't you be like everybody else?"
- "You do some of the most peculiar things."
- "Nobody else behaves like you do."
- "Nice people don't do that."
- "Most people would (or wouldn't)..."
- "What will people say if you...?"

These common expressions, which are available in a multitude of variations, are the stock-in-trade for those who want us to be more like them.

## THE BENEFITS OF CONFORMING

Why do people want us to conform? Simply put, because they are rewarded if we do. People in authority want us to be like others because then we won't confront them with unpredictable ideas and behaviors that would require them to think independently. Those who are insecure desperately want us to be like them because they see our adopting their ideas or behavior as a validation of their worth, which increases their sense of acceptance and feelings of personal security. People who feel most comfortable dealing with stereotypes are happier if we behave as they expect, because then we won't introduce any disruptive, disturbing, or unpredictable elements into their lives. And those who fear anyone who is different from them in any significant way are pleased when we are like them, because they feel least anxious when they associate with others who think and behave much as they do.

This isn't strictly a one-sided arrangement, however, because although others receive certain benefits if we decide to "fit in," so do we. For instance, if we copy established, accepted patterns of appearance and behavior we can usually avoid others' attention and criticism. If we repeat others' ideas instead of expressing our own, we feel we're less likely to sound stupid, ignorant, or naive. If we behave much as others do, we are more likely to be well-accepted and have a large circle of friends and acquaintances.

But these "benefits" of conformity possess one common denominator: *the desire to receive others' approval, or at least avoid their disapproval.* Consciously or unconsciously, we believe that if we can mimic our potential critics well enough, they'll be friendly and accepting and will provide us with the positive feedback we so desperately crave. To us, there's a direct correlation between acceptance and how well we can imitate others.

How willing are we to conform? That depends on how badly we desire approval. The greater our insecurity, the more importance we attach to fitting in. The more we depend on others' support to make us feel good about ourselves, the more agreeable we are to altering our life and personality to suit them.

## SIGNS OF CONFORMITY

How can we tell if a longing for others' approval has made us abandon our individuality? Here are some common indications:

- We change our behavior because of what we imagine others might think of it or of us
- We spend a great deal of time wondering what others think of us
- We become concerned when we discover we're behaving differently than others
- We are willing to go to extremes to avoid making people angry
- We do things not because we want to but because of the effect they will have on others
- We copy others' behaviors to try to avoid being conspicuous
- We measure success by how well we are able to please others
- We rely on external sources to guide us in most areas of our lives

## THE REAL COST OF CONFORMITY

Once we embrace conformity we become its prisoner, led through our lives by it as surely as a bull can be led by a ring through his nose. Unaware that individuality is one of our most precious assets, we become absorbed in ideas and activities that all but extinguish it.

We adopt others' goals as our own and become mindlessly involved in activities in which we have no real interest. Instead of enhancing our uniqueness, we try to smother the differences that lend richness to the fabric of life.

Since conformity values obedience more than initiative, and compliance more than intelligence, we restrict ourselves intellectually and emotionally. By duplicating others' patterns of living we become insensitive to our own choices and preferences. We live an anesthetized existence of numbing similarity and exist on a bland diet of pre-digested ideas flavored with uninspired, and often meaningless behaviors.

What is our reward for suppressing our originality? Certainly, we might have many acquaintances and feel accepted and approved of, and we may even be able to avoid blame and criticism and unwelcome attention — but at what cost? It matters little how many people accept us if we feel empty inside. In the drab, colorless world of conformity, we are an insignificant blur in a featureless society.

It is not surprising that, after spending many years engaged in dreary, imitative behavior, many of us experience what is often termed "a mid-life crisis," the sudden, shocking, and terribly depressing realization that our life has no meaning. And how could it have, when throughout the years we've marched to the beat of everyone's drum but our own? When we've lived primarily by values, ethics and ideals we've copied from others, rather than arrived at through our own reasoning. We have ignored our obligation to think for ourselves and are experiencing the inevitable outcome.

## THE JOY OF BEING DIFFERENT

Is it bad to be different? Not at all. Consider this: it isn't those who conform who receive the public's attention, but those who do not. People are fascinated with originals, and not poor copies. Who originates the trends we  follow? It isn't the people who won't do anything until they know what everybody else is doing, it is those who capitalize on an ability or characteristic that sets them apart from everyone else.

The ultimate question is, do we dare to be different? Do we have the courage to be ourselves, to swim against the tide and behave differently than others when we find their actions foolish or unrealistic? Are we brave enough to move to our own rhythm, to say no when others are saying yes, and to remain an individual when we are being pressured to merge into the crowd?

Being ourselves isn't easy, especially if conformity has been a lifelong habit. It requires us to be fearless in order to disagree with experts and challenge authorities when we feel they are wrong. We must be willing to risk criticism, ridicule, and condemnation. We must accept that our own opinion is the most important one in our world, so that we can allow others to approve or disapprove of us as heartily as they'd like.

But even if we have the inner strength to maintain our individuality and are willing to take on the world if it seeks to conform us, there are times when a little conformity is appropriate. If we wish to enjoy the company of others, as most of us do, it is impossible to avoid a certain amount of imitative behavior because similarity is the behavioral oil which lubricates our social wheels. It is important, though, that we learn to differentiate between conforming in order to get along with others and conforming because we are concerned about others' disapproval.

None of us is exactly alike. Despite surface similarities, each of us has a special viewpoint and an unmatched blend of traits and qualities that occur in no one else. We are a one-of-a-kind combination of heredity, education, and life experience, an assortment of characteristics that those who know us well identify as uniquely us. We have each been given our own song to sing, our own life-script to act out, and our own dreams to pursue. And if we wish to enjoy peace of mind, self-respect, and self-acceptance, it will not be by thinking and behaving like everyone else, but by nourishing and developing our sense of individuality,

## *Important Ideas to Consider*

- It is okay to be different from others.
- It's important to be myself.
- Real men don't worry about acting like real men.
- There's no reason for me to look, act, or think like anyone else.
- It's unnecessary for me to adopt anyone else's standards.
- It's okay to be just as I am.
- I am unique. This is not something to be either proud or ashamed of, it is merely a fact.
- I must be my own final authority and not let others do my thinking.
- Others' opinions of me are based on *their* view of reality, which may be drastically different from mine.
- I am free to accept or reject others' opinions about anything, including myself.
- Being different just to be different is merely conformity in reverse.
- No matter how I look or what I wear, some people will approve of my appearance and others will disapprove.

## *Questions to Ask Yourself*

- Do I react defensively when people criticize me?
- Do I try to change when I am criticized even though I'm not certain the criticism is valid?
- Do I think it's important to be like most other people?
- How much of what I do is done for others' approval instead of because I want to do it?
- How much do I regulate my behavior because of what people might think of me?
- Do I usually do what I believe others expect of me?

- Do I change my opinion when others disagree with me?
- If I knew no one would ever see me, how would I dress? How would I behave?
- Do I choose my clothing to please myself or because it's what is expected of me?
- Do I give gifts because I know it's expected of me and not because I want to?
- Do I often compare my appearance with others'?
- Do I often do things because "everybody does them?"
- If I felt no need for people's approval, would I be more relaxed and comfortable around others?
- How would I act if I were just "being myself?"
- How differently would I behave if I felt no need to impress anyone?
- What are some things I would do if I weren't concerned about people's opinions?

## *An Experiment*

1) List the names of five people with whom you recently carried on a conversation. If you don't know them all by name, refer to them by some other term (e.g., Bus Driver) to identify each one. Now, thinking back on these conversations, answer all these questions using the first name on your list, and then start back at the top of the list of questions with the next name on your list.

- Did I find myself saying things I didn't actually mean to _________?

- Did I exaggerate anything to improve ___________'s opinion of me?

- Did I avoid saying things I wanted to say because I was afraid
  __________ would think badly of me for saying it?

- Was I concerned about __________'s opinion of my clothing
  or general appearance?

- Was I concerned about __________'s opinion of my attrac-
  tiveness?

# CHAPTER 5

# Brian and Sally

**B**rian and his wife, Sally, were looking forward to a vacation. For the past few years Sally's parents had given them money for a trip, but this year they were short of cash and Brian and Sally had very little money of their own.

After considering a number of inexpensive possibilities, Sally suggested they go camping in a national park, and after giving the idea a little thought, Brian enthusiastically agreed. That, they both decided, would be both affordable and pleasant. They knew Sally's parents would let them use their pickup truck, so all they had to do now was borrow someone's camper.

After discussing which of their friends had a camper, they decided to ask Henry and Emma, a pleasant retired couple they'd known for several years, if they could use theirs. The older couple listened carefully the following evening when Brian and Sally asked to borrow their camper, but it was obvious the older couple had some misgivings. Finally, after what seemed like forever, Emma nodded to Henry, and Henry turned to Brian and said, "Okay."

Brian and Sally's vacation was even more pleasant than they had anticipated, but on the way home they ran into some trouble. Even though Brian was a careful driver, the heavy traffic made it impossible for him to avoid hitting a small piece of sheet metal lying on the freeway. When a tire hit it, the metal took to the air, spinning around to the right side of the pickup where it hit with a loud, ripping noise.

When they finally were able to pull off the freeway and stop, they were stunned to discover the metal had not only sliced a huge hole in the camper, it had also damaged the interior. Judging by the amount of damage, repairing it would cost quite a bit. Since they weren't well off financially, what should they do?

If you were in Brian and Sally's predicament, would you think it best to . . .

**1** tell Henry and Emma you hope their insurance will cover the repair?

**2** offer to reimburse them for the damages a little at a time?

**3** have Sally return it because they wouldn't get as angry with her?

**4** return it when Henry and Emma were gone and hope they would think the accident happened there?

**5** get a small bank loan to fix the camper?

**6** offer to split the cost of the repairs with them?

*If you chose*

**3** have Sally return it because they wouldn't get as angry with her, or

**4** return it when Henry and Emma were gone and hope they would think the accident happened there

*You perceive the problem to be* avoiding the Petries' blame.

*You think this is a problem because you believe* you'll be blamed for something that wasn't your fault.

*You believe it can best be solved by* avoiding Henry and Emma.

*PROBABLE OUTCOME:* At best, Henry and Emma will be highly doubtful that the damage occurred at their home, and at worst, extremely angry. In either case, your failing to acknowledge your responsibility in connection with the accident will alienate them from you. If they can't afford to fix the camper they'll have to forego the pleasure of using it, which will undoubtedly add to their negative feelings about you. Of course, they may use legal means to force you to pay for the damage, no matter how desperately you insist you don't have the money. There is no question, of course, about ever being able to borrow anything from them again,

*How will this make you feel?* Afraid and unhappy. Since these responses are so transparent, it's unlikely you'll be able to avoid Henry and Emma's blame. You'll be unhappy because they will almost certainly be angry with you and also because you've lost two friends, as well as the chance to borrow anything from them in the future.

*Will you feel good about yourself?* No. You'll feel guilty and ashamed because you've behaved shabbily toward Emma and Henry. In addition, behaving irresponsibly as you did lessens your self-respect and makes you feel inadequate and dependent, two characteristics not widely admired.

*For better alternatives* see the information about Answers 2 and 5.

## LEVEL 2 ANSWERS

*If you chose*

**1** tell Henry and Emma you hope their insurance will cover the repair?

**6** offer to split the cost of the repairs with them?

*You perceive the problem to be* avoiding financial responsibility for the repair.

*You think this is a problem because you believe* you should not have to handle difficult problems by yourself.

*You think it can best be solved by* getting Henry and Emma or their insurance company to pay all or part of the charges for repairing the damage.

*PROBABLE OUTCOME:* Unless Henry and Emma are pretty well off, they would probably respond cooly to your hint that they pay part of the cost of repairs. Of course, if they think fifty percent is the most they'll get from you without going to a great deal of trouble, they may accept it. More likely, though, if their insurance company won't pay for it, they'll quite reasonably decide it's *your* obligation to fix the camper since you were using it when the damage occurred. If they're unhappy with your half-hearted or non-existent offer to pay, they may take you to small claims court, in which case you'll have to pay the court costs as well as for the repairs. Although you'll undoubtedly consider the entire matter an injustice, Henry and Emma will think of it as a learning experience.

*How will this make you feel?* Angry and betrayed. Since even your offer to pay fifty percent was made reluctantly, you are angry or unhappy with Henry and Emma for insisting you pay some or all of the expense. You believe they are not the good friends you thought they were.

*Will you feel good about yourself?* No. By thinking of yourself as a victim who can't handle this problem alone, you increase your feelings of dependence and give up a little more self-respect. Worse yet, since you will pay only because you feel you *must* rather than because you understand it is your obligation to, you will not feel more generous for having done it, merely worse off than before.

*For better alternatives* see the information about Answers 2 and 5.

*If you chose*

**2** offer to reimburse them for the damages a little at a time, or

**5** get a small bank loan to fix the camper

*You perceive the problem to be* repairing the damages to Henry and Emma's camper.

*You think this is a problem because you believe* you're financially responsible for any damages that occur to property you've borrowed.

*You believe it can best be solved by* paying for the repairs yourself.

*PROBABLE OUTCOME:* You will have the camper repaired at your expense and, as a result of treating Henry and Emma fairly, will probably be on even better terms with them. Since they'll know they can trust you to be responsible for anything you might borrow, you will probably be able to use their camper again if you wish.

*How will this make you feel?* Both happy and unhappy. Needless to say, suddenly finding you have a large, unexpected expense isn't likely to make anyone happy. But in spite of that, you will be pleased because you've behaved responsibly toward the other couple, and by doing so have kept your friendship intact.

*Will you feel good about yourself?* Yes. While there are no financial advantages to behaving ethically in this situation, by treating Henry and Emma equitably, you increase your self-respect and self-esteem.

# What's The *Real* Problem

The problem isn't the hole in the camper, but who Brian and Sally will depend on to get it fixed.

It doesn't occur to the Brian and Sally of Level 1 to pay for the repairs because they suffer from the relatively common misconception that practically everyone else is better off financially than they are and, better able to suffer a loss. They consider most other adults, including Henry and Emma "grown-ups" and think of themselves as being midway on the path between infancy and maturity. If Brian and Sally had a better-developed sense of personal responsibility, they would have realized that if they had explained what happened and offered to pay for the repairs, Henry and Emma would be understanding rather than blaming.

While the Brian and Sally of Level 2 feel some responsibility, being typically Level 2 they believe a problem shared is a problem halved, especially when it's *their* problem. In this case, they feel it is best to have Henry and Emma or their insurance company pay for this unexpected expense. It is possible Henry and Emma have insurance that will cover the repair (although many people never buy insurance) but they will still have to pay the deductible amount, which can be substantial in itself.

If the problem were a mechanical one or a matter of replacing a worn-out part, it might be appropriate to ask the older couple to split the cost of repairs, but that isn't the case. From Henry and Emma's viewpoint, splitting the cost of repairs is undoubtedly better than being stuck with the entire amount. They may quite reasonably think, though, that since they had nothing to do with causing the damages, they shouldn't have to pay *anything*.

Our lives would be simplified immeasurably, no doubt, if each of us had a rich benefactor who would assume our financial burdens for us.

Unfortunately, and to our perpetual sorrow, generous, wealthy people are in such great demand that most of us must resign ourselves to paying our own way.

The Brian and Sally of Level 3 understand this. They realize that if they hadn't borrowed the camper, it would still be in Henry and Emma's yard in top-notch condition. They also realize it isn't a matter of who has the most money, but who legitimately owes the debt. Since the Brian and Sally of Level 3 try to learn from their mistakes, they may rationally decide that in the future they won't borrow anything they can't comfortably afford to insure, repair, or replace.

# Unhealthy Dependency and Becoming Fully Adult

## INDICATIONS OF DEPENDENCY

Since none of us could hope to acquire all the knowledge and skills we need for survival, we must sometimes depend on others for assistance of one sort or another and they must sometimes depend on us. We refer to this voluntary exchange of goods and services as "cooperation," which means we give people the benefit of our knowledge and skills (often in the form of money) in exchange for obtaining benefits through *their* knowledge and skills.

Dependency is a different matter altogether, however, because it refers to *unnecessary* reliance on others. In practical terms, it means that in one or more respects we wrongly consider most others stronger, richer, smarter, more capable or, in some other way, better able to do things than we are. When we are dependent, we want others to solve our problems, ease our distress, and in certain matters, care for us as a loving parent would.

Under ideal conditions, those responsible for our upbringing would have helped us develop a strong sense of independence and self-reliance as we grew older so that when we left home as a young adult, we were prepared to take care of ourselves. Unfortunately, few of us were brought up under such favorable conditions and, as a result, remain unnecessarily dependent in one or more ways.

What are some indications of this kind of dependency? Here are some common ones:

- *an unwillingness to provide our own financial support.* We see others as having more money than we have, or as being better able to earn money than we are. Because we imagine we are worse off financially than most people, no matter what our actual financial condition, we expect them to help pay our way.

- *a need for people's approval.* Uncertain about our worth as a person, we rely on others' good opinions to make us feel good about ourselves.

- *wanting others to make our decisions.* Because we mistrust our own judgment, we depend on others to tell us what to eat, how to dress, how to wear our hair, whom to marry, what career to follow, and so on, indefinitely.

- *resentment toward others.* When we rely on others to satisfy our psychological or physical needs, we become angry, indignant, and disappointed when they can't or won't.

- *considering others' needs unimportant.* Since we consider others' needs unimportant, we have little concern for how our actions might impact people's lives.

- *being self-absorbed.* Because dependency breeds insecurity, we tend to waste a large amount of time dwelling on unpleasant incidents from the past, dreaming about the future, and wondering what others really think of us and how we can get people to do what we want.

- *feeling self-pity.* Since others are rarely willing to do as much for us as we wish, we consider ourselves victims and spend a great deal of time immersed in self-pity.

All in all, this is not a list of admirable characteristics.

## DEPENDENCY ISN'T ANY FUN

While others may be inconvenienced or angered by our dependency, it has a longer-lasting, more devastating effect on us:

*We feel cheated by life.* We sacrifice numerous benefits when we depend on others. If people don't consider us accountable, we won't be trusted, which means we forfeit countless privileges and find many of life's pleasures just beyond our grasp. When we see others enjoying themselves, we feel that we're on the outside looking in and envy those "lucky" (translate that to mean "self-reliant") people who seem able to get what *we* want.

*We are often unhappy.* Our attempts to get others to take care of us often meet with failure because, unless we meet someone who feels a need to take care of us, most people will strongly resist becoming our caretakers. If they do decide to help, it is often in a way which pleases them but not necessarily us.

*We spend a lot of time blaming.* Because we typically expect more from others than they are willing to give, we are often disappointed. When our expectations fail to materialize, we complain bitterly about almost everything and everyone, except ourselves, of course. We do not blame ourselves for expecting things we're unlikely to get; it's the fault of the government, our spouse, our children, or anyone else within blaming distance.

*We must frequently resort to manipulation to get others to do what we want.* Since few volunteer when our cry for help goes out, it's often up to us to persuade someone to come to our aid. We wheedle, cajole, beg, and implore. We resort to threats, intimidation, anger, tears, or any other kind of emotional prodding we think might get us the help we believe we need.

*We dehumanize those we depend on.* When we rely on others to achieve our ends for us we think of them less as fellow human beings than as objects we can manipulate or sources of supply. Because this attitude automatically inhibits friendship, openness, and trust, we find it impossible to develop healthy, pleasant, and long-lasting friendships and relationships.

*We must sometimes do an enormous amount of work to convince others to help us.* At times, we have to invest as much time and energy in trying to persuade people to do things as we would in learning to do them ourselves. Because people hesitate to assume responsibility for our problems, getting their assistance can be a real struggle. Also, some of those whose help we seek have dependency problems of their own and are looking to *us* as a source of help!

*We experience a lot of anxiety.* Relying on others to do things for us is at best a chancy proposition. Because most people stay pretty busy satisfying their own wants and needs, we must always wonder whether they'll have time for ours. How can we not worry when so much of our future depends on others instead of ourselves?

*People tend to avoid us.* How do those we depend on feel about our relying on them? Because most people get tired of continually being on the giving end of a relationship, they become resentful and may try to avoid us entirely. When we expect too much from others, we sometimes end up with nothing.

*We restrict our personal freedom.* Dependency and lack of freedom go hand in hand. When we rely on others to help us, we are not allowed to live as we wish. To the extent that we want people's help, we must behave as they wish us to in certain respects. If we do not, their help is likely to be withdrawn.

***We sacrifice our self-respect and self-esteem.*** Dependency has a disastrous effect on our feelings about ourselves. Because many of us equate our ability to do things with our value as a person, the more we must ask others to do for us, the more we drop in our own estimation.

But troubling as these problems are, our greatest loss is in terms of maturity: ***To the extent that we are dependent, we remain emotionally immature and never become fully adult.*** Instead of enjoying the pleasures and responsibilities of adults, we must suffer many of the indignities of children, either trying to please others or throwing a tantrum to get what we want. And each time we must beg others for help, we unconsciously reinforce the belief that we are weak, helpless, and inadequate.

## OVERCOMING DEPENDENCY

How can we reverse this harmful pattern and transform a leaning, dependent attitude into one of self-reliance? By attaining greater understanding and changing our attitude, and then by

- doing as much as we possibly can for ourselves and calling on others for help only when a task is literally beyond us

- investing more energy in solving our problems than in soliciting help

- realizing that although we don't come into this world with self-reliance, we *do* bring an inherent capacity for it

- understanding that we are dependent, not because we lack the ability to do things for ourselves, but because we have not yet developed our skills

- recognizing that we have no alternative but to accept adult responsibilities if we want the privileges that go with them

- focusing on our own problem-solving abilities and what *we* can do, rather than trying to get others to do things for us

- concentrating on our strengths instead of our weaknesses

- realizing that no one, including ourselves is entitled to a free ride

- internalizing the fact that *we* are responsible for providing for our needs, just as others are for theirs and that it is no one's job to take care of us

- thinking of others as independent equals rather than as our caretakers.

We cannot move forward, of course, without some growing pains. To emerge from dependency, we must re-evaluate the beliefs that encourage us to think there is genuine benefit in remaining dependent. Instead of continuing the self-limiting thoughts that make us lean on others, we need to replace them with positive ideas that emphasize our own skills. Rather than thinking of ourselves as incapable, helpless, or weak, we need to acknowledge and emphasize our strengths. And as we take part in this process, we will develop and use previously ignored or unrecognized abilities and stretch our minds and broaden our viewpoints.

Does becoming self-reliant sound like an overly ambitious project, with too many risks and too few rewards? It is anything but. When we are independent, we feel free, and life is a joyous celebration in which we enthusiastically participate.

Developing healthy self-reliance isn't an overnight process, of course, and like any other skill, we will be better at using it some times than others. If a temporary failure makes us feel like slipping back into dependency, we need to keep in mind that, although becoming self-reliant requires effort, *so does remaining dependent.* If we cling to a self-limiting viewpoint, we must continually re-decide to think like a child rather than an adult; we must go on entreating others to help us and resigning ourselves to disappointment when they do not. And since we must choose between investing our energy in either self-reliance *or* dependency, why not take the path that promises the greatest freedom and the richest rewards?

While there is no question that self-reliance is an essential requirement for success and happiness, it is unrealistic to think we must be entirely self-sufficient because, practically speaking, this is impossible. Part of becoming fully adult is realizing that when matters require a skill we don't possess or knowledge we don't have and can't reasonably acquire, we must unashamedly turn to others for help, but always with the understanding that we will be required to pay for their help in one way or another.

If we are accustomed to leaning on others, it can take much courage to decide to free ourselves from dependency. When we finally make that decision, we may experience a brief, but highly disturbing, moment when it feels as though the bottom has fallen out of the universe. When this happens, we will question the wisdom of our decision and anxiously wonder, "Am I being foolish to relinquish an attitude that has served me so often in the past?" But once we have met that moment and it is behind us, we will realize with newfound clarity that, rather than giving up something of value by letting go of dependency, we are discarding only some outgrown remnants of childhood.

## Important Ideas to Consider

- I learn nothing about doing things when they are done for me.
- If I expect to receive from others, I must be prepared to give in return.
- It is my job to take care of myself.
- If I try to escape my legitimate financial obligations, my attitude may limit my earning power and keep me from making financial progress.
- By emphasizing what I *don't* have, I reinforce my belief that I will never have enough, no matter how much I may actually have.
- By using my ability to change and improve, I can stop being dependent and can experience the pleasure of self-sufficiency.
- Since none of us ever reaches our full potential, I can continue to grow as a person as long as I live.
- If I think of myself as someone who never has enough money, I will develop a "shortage consciousness," which means that even though I might have everything I need and more, I will never feel as though I have enough.

## Questions to Ask Yourself

- Do I become frustrated or angry with others when they do not give me what I want?
- Do I depend on people to introduce themselves to me because I am too shy to introduce myself?
- Do I expect others to keep me from being unhappy or bored?

- Do I depend on others to love me because I don't love myself enough?
- Do I think of myself as a strong, powerful adult or a weak, helpless child? Why?
- Do I consider myself a giver or a receiver?
- Am I a person who does things or one who expects things to be done for me?
- Do I enjoy the good things in life or just envy those who do?
- Do I feel uncomfortable when I have to make decisions?

# CHAPTER 6

# Richard and His Father

Ever since Richard was a child, he had known his father expected him to become a doctor. Richard's father was a physician, and his grandfather and great-grandfather had been, too, and Richard knew his dad expected him to carry on the family tradition. In fact, just days after Richard was born, his father made a substantial contribution to the medical school from which he'd graduated to guarantee Richard a place there when he was old enough to attend. As his father planned it, once Richard completed his medical training, they would become partners. Then Richard could take over the entire practice when his father was ready to retire,. Anticipating the future, Richard's father had already had a brass nameplate made with both their names on it.

Sharing a practice with his father sounded okay to Richard. Since they usually got along fairly well, he thought they could work together easily enough. Richard didn't find medicine as fascinating as his dad did, but from what he'd seen, it was financially rewarding.

Once Richard completed high school, he entered the university his father had attended, and as soon as he could, took preliminary medical classes. During his second year, needing an elective course, he chose one in archaeology, a subject about which he knew practically nothing.

The course was a revelation to Richard; as he learned about ancient civilizations and read about the work of earlier archaeologists, an exciting, enticing new world opened up for him. Archaeology, he decided, was so fascinating that he could spend the rest of his life involved in it. He knew it wouldn't pay nearly as well as medicine, but he wouldn't mind if he was doing work he loved.

To make sure his new interest wasn't just temporary, Richard signed up for more archaeology classes whenever he could and even participated in some small "digs" not far from the university. Rather than boring him, these experiences only increased his appetite for more.

But one day reality set in. "Who am I fooling?" he asked himself, as with a sinking heart, he realized his father would never agree to his switching careers. His father was determined that Richard would be a physician and he would be extremely angry and hurt if his son suggested pursuing any other career.

If you were Richard, for the best of all concerned, would you . . .

**1** become a physician and take long vacations to do archaeological work?

**2** pursue a career in archaeology, even though it's certain your father will be extremely upset?

**3** go along with your father's plans to avoid making him unhappy?

**4** try to talk your father into letting you switch careers?

**5** get your medical degree and take up archaeology when your father dies?

*If you chose*

**1** become a physician and take long vacations to do archaeological digs, *or*

**3** go along with his plans to avoid making him unhappy, *or*

**5** get your medical degree and take up archaeology when your father passes on

*You perceive the problem to be* avoiding upsetting your father.

*You think this is a problem because you believe* it's more important to please your father than yourself.

*You believe it can best be solved by* doing as your father wishes.

*PROBABLE OUTCOME:* You will get your medical degree, join your father's practice, and find that you've plenty to do as it is without taking time off for archaeological activities. Any Level 1 solution will please your father, of course, because you'll be doing what he wants you to do. You, however, instead of having a life of your own, will end up with a warmed-over version of your father's and you'll probably wonder until you die how different your life would have been if you had pursued archaeology.

*How is this likely to make you feel?* At first you'll just feel disappointed, but after a while frustration, resentment, anger, and bitterness will take over. Eventually you'll come to resent your father's interference, no matter how accepting of it you may have been initially. And since you're not particularly enthusiastic about practicing medicine, you'll spend most of your time engaged in work that will give you little or no pleasure.

**Will you feel good about yourself?** No. If you have the intelligence required to become a physician, you will certainly realize in later life that you allowed yourself to be victimized and manipulated out of choosing a career you'd enjoy.

*For a better alternative see* the information about Answer 2.

**LEVEL 2 ANSWER**

*If you chose*

**4** try to talk your father into letting you switch careers

**You perceive the problem to be** getting what you want without alienating your father.

**You think this is a problem because you believe** it's important your father approve of your career choice.

**You think it can best be solved by** persuading him you should be an archaeologist instead of a physician.

*PROBABLE OUTCOME:* It is not inconceivable that this kind of response *could* work, but considering that your father has charted your career practically from beginning to end, it's almost impossible to imagine him graciously giving in to your request. It's more likely you'll encounter strong-willed, stubborn, and possibly bitter opposition. Since what you want conflicts with his cherished plans, he'll probably do or say anything that he thinks will make you change your mind.

*How is this likely to make you feel?* Disappointed, frustrated, resentful, and uncertain. You'll be extremely unhappy and resentful because he wouldn't agree to your request. His insistence that you enter the field of medicine makes you wonder which is most important to him: your happiness or your choice of career.

*Will you feel good about yourself?* No. Because your attempt to convince your father is doomed to failure, you'll feel victimized when he doesn't agree with your plan. You will also feel inadequate, believing you might have succeeded if you'd presented your case more skillfully.

*For a better alternative* see the information about Answer 2.

**LEVEL 3 ANSWER**

*If you chose*

**2** pursue the career you think you'll enjoy, even though your father may be unhappy?

*You perceive the problem to be* having allowed your father to make an extremely important decision for you.

*You think this is a problem because you have realized* it is your right, not his, to choose your career.

*You believe it can best be solved by* explaining to him that you must do what *you* feel is best for you, even though he might disagree.

*PROBABLE OUTCOME:* Because you've decided fulfilling your own dream is more important than fulfilling your father's, you will continue your education in archaeology and make it your career, and your father will be disappointed. If he chooses not to pay for the rest of your studies, you may have to support yourself while going to school. If he is willing to acknowledge your right to make choices for yourself, he will probably continue to finance your education, although not with as much enthusiasm as he would if you were obtaining a medical degree. When you have completed your degree(s), you will go on to do the archaeological work you enjoy.

*How is this likely to make you feel?* Regretful, concerned, and then happy. You will feel apprehensive about breaking the news to your father, but you will be relieved when you have done it. Pursuing your chosen career will bring you great pleasure.

*Will you feel good about yourself?* Yes. Although you may be uncomfortable to begin with, the satisfaction of assuming control of your life and doing work you enjoy will minimize and finally eliminate your discomfort.

# What's the *Real* Problem?

Richard is in a particularly difficult position: while he desperately wants to become an archeologist, he is afraid that doing so will cost him his father's emotional (and possibly financial) support.

Despite the possibilities suggested by the Level 1 approaches, Richard's problem is not that of keeping his father happy. This is fortunate because it's almost certain the elder Hughes will become upset when Richard mentions wanting to become an archeologist instead of a physician.

Nor, as the Level 2 answer suggests, is Richard's dilemma that of convincing his father to let him become an archaeologist. While it is commendable of him to want to spare his father's feelings, Richard's concern is badly misplaced. In making decisions of major importance, such as selecting a career, it is *his own* feelings he must consider because *he* is the one who will have to live with the consequences of his decision.

As the Richard of Level 3 realized, the real problem is not keeping his father happy; it is deciding who is going to make one of the most important decisions in his life. Should he let his father (or anyone, for that matter) persuade him to enter a career that will bring him small satisfaction? Or to state it differently, should he consider his father's happiness more important than his own?

The Level 3 Richard understands that if his father becomes angry or unhappy, that is his father's problem, not his. Presumably, Dr. Hughes had the opportunity to select the career *he* wanted. If he did not, and allowed someone to select it for him, that was *his* choice and certainly no justification for inflicting similar damage on his son.

Will Dr. Hughes refuse to continue financing Richard's education as a result of his career choice? If he does, it is obvious that Richard's happiness is less important to him than gratifying his desire. Parents who love their children and respect their rights and individuality don't try to turn them into miniature versions of themselves, nor do they try to make their major life decisions for them.

If Richard is certain archaeology will continue to be his ruling passion, then in the interest of personal integrity and happiness, he should let no one, no matter how close, talk him out of making it his career. And considering his lukewarm attitude toward the field of medicine, wouldn't it be best for both him and his prospective patients if he became a devoted archaeologist rather than an indifferent or negligent physician?

People in Richard's position need to keep in mind that others are free to expect anything they like of us, but we are not compelled to make their expectations reality. In the words of a song familiar to many of us, "You can't please everyone, so you've got to please yourself."

# Taking Charge

An amazing number of people would like to manage our lives for us, or at the very least, make some of our key decisions. Why? Motives tend to overlap but generally because it is to their advantage in one or more ways. Some seek to influence us because they enjoy feeling in control, while others genuinely (but often incorrectly) believe we need their help. There are also those who want us to do as they suggest because our doing so will help them achieve objectives of their own, such as confirmation of their own beliefs or an affirmation of their "rightness," or, as in the case of the advertising industry, because it will put more money in their pockets.

By far the largest group of would-be advisors consists of those who have an unjustifiably high opinion of their own knowledge or wisdom and an unjustifiably low opinion of ours. Like Richard's father, they assume they know what is right and best for others, and if they think it appropriate for us to do a particular thing, then that is what they believe we must do. Not surprisingly, many of these people take jobs in government or religion, occupying positions in which they try to create rules they believe will protect us, not just from evil-doers, but from ourselves!

The techniques of those who would influence us vary as much as their motives. Some use a subtle approach, telling us what they expect of us or offering hints, recommendations, or advice. If these tactics fail, they may nag, complain, cry, try to induce guilt, or even threaten to have a nervous breakdown. Those who feel they have a unique insight into right and wrong may bring up morals, religious doctrines, the concept of fairness, or any other pre-digested idea they feel might convince us of the rightness of the action they suggest. A few individuals (usually those with whom we've had a close relationship) will point out how much they've done for us, indicating we owe them something for the time, money, or energy they've invested in us.

Often we can identify people with this unfortunate tendency by phrases or sentences they typically use:

> "I only want what's best for you."
>
> "You'll thank me for this later."
>
> "The smartest thing for you to do is…"
>
> "If I were you, I'd…
>
> "I just want to help."
>
> "Don't you think you should…?"
>
> "Most people would…"
>
> "You ought to…"
>
> "It's the proper thing to do."

Experienced users of remarks like these try to make them seem like moral imperatives that we *must* obey, rather than the mere suggestions they actually are.

## WHY WE TAKE OTHERS' ADVICE

If we have allowed others to make our decisions and later regretted it, we must understand that those who seek to influence us can be villains only with our permission. And just as those who would like to make our decisions have reasons for wanting to, we have reasons for letting them:

> ***We trust people's ideas because we believe they like us.*** When we think people have a sincere interest in our welfare, we feel treasured and cared for, which makes us inclined to uncritically accept and act on their suggestions.

*We lack confidence in our own decision-making skills.* If we consider our knowledge or experience too limited or our mental equipment less reliable than others', we welcome help in making decisions because we believe other people are better qualified to make them than we are.

*We want to avoid blame.* If we act on our own decisions and things don't work out, we will have no one to blame but ourselves. If, on the other hand, we let *others* decide what we should do, we can always blame them if anything goes wrong.

*We want people to be happy.* When we believe our actions have the power to affect others' emotions and moods, we may be deterred from doing what we'd really like to do because we're afraid people will respond negatively to our decision. Our unspoken motto is "Their happiness is more important than mine."

*We are afraid of people's anger.* We all know people who try to use anger as an emotional bludgeon to beat others into emotional submission. If we are unwilling to do what these people want, they attack with temper-tantrums, hurt feelings, the "silent treatment," or other unpleasant emotions.

*We feel less pressured when we let others make our decisions.* When having to make decisions makes us tense and nervous, it feels good to just relax and let others make our choices for us. If we do, we can avoid the uncomfortable indecision that ordinarily troubles us.

*We want to avoid feeling guilty or ashamed.* At times we let people convince us we have an obligation to them, even when we do not. Believing this, however, we do what they expect us to, in order to escape the guilt and shame we'd feel otherwise.

*We lack experience in making decisions.* If we feel we have not had the opportunity to develop our own problem-solving abilities, we think we must rely on others to help with our decisions..

*We feel it's appropriate for others to decide for us.* If we were raised in an authoritarian household or by dictatorial parents, it does not occur to us to question the wisdom of being advised by others.

None of these reasons, no matter how convincing they might sound, is valid.

## THE DISADVANTAGES TO LETTING OTHERS GUIDE US

"But," we may be thinking, "if I want to be advised, and others want to advise me, what could be more perfect?" And truly, this arrangement does sound like the proverbial "marriage made in heaven." But no garden exists without a serpent or two. Although this kind of arrangement might seem mutually beneficial to begin with, inevitably, letting others do our thinking works against us because *the ability to think for ourselves is the key to success in every area of our life.*

This is why we must stand firm when others try to exert control over our future. If we do not, the disadvantages are many:

*We never learn to make decisions ourselves.* Allowing others to guide us denies us the experience we need when, inevitably, we are forced to make decisions on our own. When we allow others to make our decisions, we become so accustomed to being helped that we soon feel incapable of making decisions ourselves. Rather than feeling at ease and self-assured, we wonder what to do, what to say, and in some cases, even what to think.

*We weaken and blur our sense of self.* When we work to achieve goals we have chosen only to please others, our individuality fades and grows dimmer. By following others' directions, we let them "create" us, and we become what *they* want us to be instead of what *we* want to become. And if we are what others have made us, we cannot possibly be ourselves.

*We lose self-respect and self-esteem.* In trying to earn others' approval by doing what they suggest, we deny ourselves the right to have goals and values of our own. In neglecting our needs in this manner, we inflict both emotional and mental damage on ourselves. By giving others' wishes and needs a higher priority than ours, we deny our self-worth and diminish ourselves in our own eyes.

*We subject ourselves to an emotional beating.* On one hand, we're afraid people will have bad feelings about us if we behave contrary to their wishes, and on the other, we feel trapped and resentful because we've allowed others to take control of our life.

*We can be easily manipulated.* When fear of another's anger or negative emotions deters us from doing something that is our right to do, or if we can maintain close relationships only by giving in to others' viewpoints, we are allowing ourselves to be manipulated. Or to put it another way, people do not treat us as a fellow human being but as an object to be used in whatever fashion most pleases them.

*We can act on some pretty bad advice.* People who believe they are wise enough to run others' lives are not only wrong, they're dangerous. Ironically, persons whose own lives are a shambles often feel qualified to offer us suggestions about improving ours.

How do the minor benefits we receive from letting others decide for us measure up to the disadvantages we incur? No matter how we look at it, any advantages we receive are from it are strictly temporary, while the disadvantages may remain with us forever.

## NOW UNDER NEW MANAGEMENT

If we have allowed others to assume dominance in our decision-making, how can we regain control? We can begin slowly and systematically by first understanding that self-direction is our right and then by taking one small step after another until we have developed *our own* sense of what is right and appropriate.

Conflicting feelings may make developing independence difficult for everyone concerned: difficult for us, because we *do* want to make our own decisions, but we also want to enjoy the freedom of *not* having to make them. Those who have been making our decisions would probably be relieved if we learned to make our own, but they are averse to giving up the pleasant, ego-caressing sensations of control and indispensability.

Uncomfortable or not, however, for the sake of future happiness we must cultivate the ability to stand on our own feet, make our own decisions, and create our own master-plan for the future. If others are unwilling to encourage our independence, we must set forth boldly and do it ourselves. Cruel and callous though it may seem, in order to do what is best for ourselves, we must sometimes behave in ways which displease others. If some react to our growing self-sufficiency with anger or unhappiness, we must keep in mind that their feelings are a choice, not an inevitability, and base our decisions on what seems best to us rather than on how others may react to them.

It is only reasonable that our important personal decisions should be made by us and not by others who may place their own interests ahead of ours. If a decision is to be right for us, it must be based on *our own* informed judgment. While people's counsel may make us aware of other options, accepting others' ideas without examining them from the viewpoint of *our own* feelings and ideas can do us incalculable harm because they're based on someone else's ideas of what's best.

No matter how lovingly it has been fashioned, it's unwise to try to force ourselves into a mold created by another. The only thing more tragic than realizing that others have made some of our major decisions is having to live with the results of those decisions.

Those who respect our rights and individuality don't try to force their will on us, nor do they want to be our caretakers; they want what is best for us. They realize we must be allowed to make our own decisions, even if that sometimes means making mistakes, because they understand we will be the wiser for making them.

Regardless of how convincingly others may argue that their ideas for us are best, it is *our* right to plan our life, not anyone else's, including our nearest and dearest. Unless we are literally incapable of making our own choices, we should give no one the right to make them for us.

## *Important Ideas to Consider*

- My decisions are my responsibility.
- My opinions are as important as those of anyone else.
- Other people create their own emotions, just as I do.
- Family members are people first, and family second.
- Being well-liked is poor compensation for not being able to live as I choose.
- I am the person best qualified to make my important decisions.
- I do not have to compromise myself just to please others.

- If I have to suffer for someone's mistakes, I'd rather they were my own.
- My life is my responsibility.

## Questions to Ask Myself

- Do I allow people to make my decisions *for* me, instead of *with* me?
- Would I rather have others make my decisions than make them myself?
- Do I believe important decisions are best left up to others?
- Am I afraid to express an unpopular opinion?
- Do I sometimes feel everyone but me has a say in what happens in my life?
- Am I more concerned about others' feelings than I am about my own?
- Do I feel family relationships automatically create obligations?
- Am I more concerned about others liking me than I am about living as I'd like?
- Do I do unpleasant or undesirable things just to make others happy?
- Will other people's decisions work for me?
- Do people find it easy to "manage" me?

## An Experiment

Let's examine some aspects of your life to find out if you've been sacrificing self-determination for emotional peace. Armed with a piece of paper and a pencil or pen, ask yourself the following questions and write down your answers. There may be more than one answer for some questions.

1) Who chooses most of my clothing?

2) Who chose the home/apartment I live in?

3) Whose idea was it for me to have the job I have?

4) Does anyone other than me choose what I read?

5) Who usually decides which movies I'll see?

6) Who selects the music I listen to?

7) Do I make my own vacation plans, or does someone else?

8) Do I let advertising agencies make some of my decisions?

If you find that you are not the person who makes most of these decisions, it might be time for a long, hard look at your life, and a re-evaluation of your decision-making processes.

# CHAPTER 7

# Mikki and Paul

**M**ikki thought her friend Leanne was joking when she told her that Paul, another student in the art class Mikki and Leanne were taking, thought Mikki was a terrible snob. According to Leanne, Paul thought Mikki acted as though she were better than everyone else. Leanne, who had known Paul since high school, had run into him at a grocery store a few days ago. While discussing the class the three of them shared, he expressed his opinion of Mikki at some length. In fact, Leanne said, he seemed more interested in criticizing Mikki  than in talking about the art class.

Paul, Mikki  recalled, was a tall, rather slender young man who rarely seemed to smile. Mikki had never talked to him in class, not because she was standoffish, but simply because she and Leanne sat at the opposite end of the spacious classroom from him. And in a class as large as theirs, there simply wasn't time to get acquainted with everyone. In fact, the only reason Mikki could even identify Paul was because the instructor held roll call at the beginning of each class session.

Mikki was perplexed by Paul's comment. She considered herself friendly, and no one else had ever accused her of being conceited or aloof. What had she done, she wondered uneasily, to make him think she was unsociable? Have I unknowingly been giving people the wrong idea about me? she asked herself. And if I have, what should I do about the poor impression I seem to have made on Paul?

If you were in Mikki's place would you , , ,

**1** sit near Paul during the next class, so you can talk with him and let him know he's wrong?

**2** invite him out for coffee, so he can get to know what you're really like?

**3** don't be unfriendly toward him, but let him think whatever he chooses about you?

**4** apologize for accidentally giving him the wrong impression?

**5** behave toward him as you do to everyone else in class?

*If you chose*

**4** apologize for accidentally giving him the wrong impression

*You perceive the problem to be* that you're doing something that makes people think badly of you.

*You think this is a problem because you believe* it's important to keep others pleased with you and your behavior, or at least not unhappy about them.

*You believe it can best be solved by* making an effort to be friendlier to Paul.

*PROBABLE OUTCOME:* You will go out of your way to be agreeable to Paul and after you've demonstrated how friendly you are, you'll ask what made him think you were a snob. Then, since you regard displeasing others as a serious matter, you will try to change whatever aspect of your personality or behavior he indicates needs some improvement.

*How is this likely to make you feel?* Unhappy, guilty, inadequate, insecure, and uncertain. You'll feel bad because you think you've failed at a basic and relatively simple task, that of behaving amiably toward others. And if you fail at something so easy, you wonder if perhaps you shouldn't also question your judgment and adequacy in regard to other aspects of your life (if, that is, you do not mistrust them already).

*Will you feel good about yourself?* No. When you choose this kind of answer, in effect you say, "Others' opinions are more important than mine." By accepting Paul's criticism at face value you acknowledge his judgment and opinions to be superior to your own, which means you also consider him superior to you. Comparing yourself with him makes you doubt your intelligence and ideas and negatively assess your value and personal importance. To the extent that you take Paul's (or anyone's) remarks about you to heart, you allow them to dictate, not just your feelings about yourself, but your emotions.

*For better alternatives* see the information about Answers 3 and 5.

## LEVEL 2 ANSWERS

*If you chose*

**1** sit near Paul during the next class, so you can talk with him and let him know he's wrong, or

**2** invite him out for coffee, so he can get to know what you're really like

*You perceive the problem to be* Paul's mistaken impression of you.

*You think this is a problem because you believe* it's important that others not have incorrect ideas about you.

*You believe it can best be solved by* showing him how wrong he is.

*PROBABLE OUTCOME:* You will make a point of introducing yourself to Paul because you're positive that once he is acquainted with the "real" you, he'll discover how mistaken he was in his judgment. Once you get to know him you'll find he is an awkward and uncomfortable companion and not the kind of person with whom you could enjoy a mutually rewarding friendship.

*How is this likely to make you feel?* Concerned and embarrassed at first, and finally, disappointed. Initially, you will be distressed because you believe Paul has an erroneous impression of you. You'll feel much better once you believe you've corrected his mistake. However, you will find that people who make unfounded judgments as he has do not make particularly pleasant friends.

*Will you feel good about yourself?* No. Although you'll no doubt congratulate yourself when you first get Paul "straightened out," Once you get acquainted with him, you'll discover that getting involved with him was a mistake and question your judgment.

*For better alternatives* see the information about Answers 3 and 5.



*If you chose*

**3** don't be unfriendly toward him, but let him think whatever he chooses about you, or

**5** behave toward him as you do to everyone else in class

*You realize there is no problem* unless you create one by becoming concerned about a relative stranger's opinion of you.

*You think this is <u>not</u> a problem because you believe* it is not necessary for everyone to approve of you, especially people you've never met.

*You believe there is no problem* to solve.

*PROBABLE OUTCOME:* You will continue to attend and enjoy the art class.

*How is this likely to make you feel?* Compassionate, understanding, and pleased. You understand that Paul's comments were probably *not* made because he thought you acted snobbish, but for other reasons. You will feel pleased because you did not create a problem by becoming concerned about his expressed opinion.

*Will you feel good about yourself?* Yes. Because you've chosen to value your own opinion of yourself more than someone else's. Relying on your inner authority in this manner reaffirms your belief in *your own* opinion and judgment, especially when the alternative is accepting the opinion of someone you don't know.

# What's the *Real* Problem?

Despite Paul's comments, the central issue in this chapter is not Mikki's friendliness or lack of it. It is whether Mikki, who has never met Paul, should be concerned enough about his negative opinion of her to try to change it.

While those who chose Level 1 or Level 2 approaches felt it necessary to take action in response to Paul's accusations, the Mikki who chose a Level 3 answer thinks it would be a waste of time. Since she hasn't knowingly been unfriendly to Paul and has never before been told she is snobbish, she thinks it likely that Paul used this common manipulative ploy hoping Leanne would repeat his comments and Mikki would introduce herself to prove how wrong he was.

Ultimately, Mikki's response depends on how badly she desires his approval and to what lengths she will go to get it. If she believes his opinion is important she'll try to persuade him that friendliness oozes from her every pore. If she is mature enough to realize that someone she doesn't know is unlikely to be a good judge of her character, she'll give Paul's comments the attention they deserve, which is practically none. Since she doesn't take Paul's criticism seriously, she feels no need to refute his accusations.

Although it might seem kind for Mikki to make an overture to Paul if she thinks he used this strategy because he is shy, would it be? Shyness is totally curable, and Paul won't become more secure if she accepts and rewards his insecure behavior. If he *is* shy and Mikki tries to compensate for it by introducing herself, she'll strengthen his belief that using manipulation is preferable to a direct, adult-to-adult approach.

Wouldn't it be wise of Mikki to give Paul's allegations some thought, in case they might be true? Perhaps, but consider the circumstances: Paul, who has never met or talked to Mikki, has accused her of being a snob. If he had introduced himself and she was rude or rebuffed him, it might be good to give his statements some thought. He didn't, however, and since he is the only one who has made this assertion, she has no reason to modify her behavior in response to it. The only problem that needs to be solved is Paul's and he must solve it himself.

# Wanting People to Like Us



*"For what care I who calls me well or ill...?"*
WILLIAM SHAKESPEARE, Sonnet 112

**U**nless we were brought up in exceptional circumstances, we undoubtedly suffer from the incorrect belief that others' approval of us is not only important in itself, but is essential to our psychological well-being. While there is a shred of truth in this, for the most part people's opinions of us are unimportant.

This is not to say that having others' approval cannot be pleasant, because it can, and we would be perverse creatures indeed if we didn't prefer being liked to being disliked. Here is the point, though: a mere *preference* for approval won't usually cause problems, but when the desire for approval is the dominant force behind our actions and we will do anything we must to win others' acceptance, we are in for a great deal of trouble.

*We lose our sense of individuality.* To the extent that we allow people's approval or disapproval to influence our behavior, we cease to exist as individuals and become a committee project, a creature defined and molded by others' wishes. As an inevitable consequence of this self-denial and self-abasement, we become nonpersons, shadowy, spiritless reflections of those who have shaped us. The more we defer to others, the weaker grows our sense of self-identity.

*We diminish our self-esteem.* Each time we modify our opinions or behavior purely to please others, we unconsciously rank ourselves below them in importance and intrinsic worth, reinforcing our belief that we don't really amount to much. By trying to be what others wish us to be, we erode our feelings of self-worth and demonstrate our belief that we are not likable and worthwhile as we are.

*We sacrifice integrity and self-respect.* Unwilling to risk others' displeasure, we say things we don't believe and avoid contradicting people or expressing ideas of our own. Striving to offend no one, we behave in ways that feel unnatural and uncomfortable. Although consciously we may be unaware of the effects of our bowing and scraping, each time we act to please others instead of ourselves our store of self-honesty and self-respect shrinks a little more.

*We become slaves to those we feel we must please.* When we rely on people's approval to feel good about ourselves, we are susceptible to their manipulation. When those whose approval we value urge us to do things we're reluctant to do, they have only to threaten to withdraw their approval and we meekly fall into line. This kind of groveling, besides being highly unpleasant, is servitude degrading to everyone involved.

*We are susceptible to emotional whiplash.* If we feel good about ourselves only when others seem to, we are highly vulnerable emotionally; since we can't control people's thoughts, we can't control how we feel about ourselves. As long as we allow others' feelings to dictate *our* feelings, instead of enjoying a comfortable emotional balance, we will fly about on an emotional roller-coaster propelled by others' moods and fancies.

**INDICATIONS OF APPROVAL-SEEKING**

How can we tell if we want people's approval too much? Here are some of the symptoms:

- We display a greatly edited version of ourselves to others because we're afraid they won't like us if they find out what we're *really* like.

- We do our utmost to avoid doing or saying anything that might offend, annoy, or anger anyone.

- We spend much of our time trying to prove to others that we're worthwhile human beings.

- We adjust our behavior to suit our associates' moods instead of our own.

- We change our opinion if others disagree with us.

- We apologize for anything bad that happens, including things over which we had no control.

- We try to impress others with who we are, what we can do, what we own, or who we know.

- We accept rude treatment and bad service because we're afraid of making someone angry.

- We feel compelled to straighten out any misconceptions of us that we believe people have.

- We tell people what we think they want to hear instead of what we want to say.

- We choose our actions with an eye toward pleasing as many people as possible.

Obviously, trying to make others think well of us makes for an extremely restricted life. And considering the many disadvantages of wanting others' approval and how miserable we make ourselves trying to get it, why aren't we working diligently to eliminate this harmful problem once and for all? Well, as peculiar as it sounds, we do nothing about this problem because *we **don't know it exists.***

Oh, of course we do become angry when we feel we have no choice but to please others, and we *do* feel resentful and bitter and emotionally beaten-up because of it. But instead of recognizing these feelings as the symptoms of approval-seeking they are, we think there is something wrong with us for experiencing them. Nothing is, of course, *except* that we have grossly over-valued others' approval.

Just how much *are* people's good opinions worth? ***Unless people have something we want and we must have their approval to get it, their good opinion is worthless.*** It is shocking but true: ***others' approval has no intrinsic value and it is not worth having for its own sake.*** Unless approval puts food on our table, a roof over our head, or money in our bank account, it is not a necessity but an option.

## ELIMINATING THE NEED FOR APPROVAL

There are two changes we must make if we want to avoid this degrading behavior. First, ***we must improve our opinion of ourselves.*** The only reason we seek others' approval is that we do not yet provide enough of our own, or to state it differently, the more approval we grant ourselves, the less we look for it elsewhere.

Second, ***we must learn to differentiate between needing approval and wanting it.*** We *need* the approval of only those who can exercise control over our lives and those who provide things we need for survival. If others' approval does not bring with it any concrete benefits, then we want it only to feel better about ourselves. Be clear on this: There is a great difference between pleasing people to assure our freedom and survival, and pleasing them just to make them like us.

## FREEDOM FROM SEEKING APPROVAL

We may run into some opposition when we decide to give our own approval top priority. Some may cheer us on while others will try to discourage us. Those who do not encourage our independence will object because as long as we are concerned about their approval, we are easily manipulated. When we begin valuing our own approval more than theirs, they may call us selfish, uncaring, inconsiderate, or mean. We can usually translate this to mean "I'm losing control over you and I don't like it."

In the interest of common sense, however, since we have little power over others' actions and still less over their thoughts, why do we not avoid a lot of unnecessary emotional wear-and-tear and simply let people think whatever they want? Since most of us are already subjected to large amounts of unavoidable stress, why make matters worse by attaching excessive and unwarranted importance to people's opinions?

Once we have rid ourselves of the erroneous notion that others' good opinions are important in themselves, we will no longer feel it necessary to make special efforts to please. When people give us sincere compliments, we can accept and enjoy their approval without considering it essential. While we won't be insensitive to others' opinions about us, we will use them neither as criteria for rating ourselves, nor as emotional bludgeons with which to beat ourselves. When people criticize us we will filter their comments through the screen of our personal values, and then act on or discard them as we deem appropriate. If people ask for our frank opinion, we will give it without trying to disguise our real feelings. And best of all, remaining centered in healthy self-approval, we will steadily pursue our course without being buffeted about by the winds of praise and blame.

# *Important Ideas to Consider*

- Unless I have entered into a contract with others, I don't have to please anyone but myself.
- People's good opinions don't make me a better person, nor do their bad opinions make me a worse one.
- Other people's approval is less important than my own.
- People cannot look down on me unless I look up to them.
- Being well-liked is poor compensation for not being able to live as I choose.
- I am not obligated to prove people are wrong if they have incorrect ideas about me.
- People are welcome to believe anything they like about me.
- If everyone on earth thinks I'm wonderful but *I* don't, I'll still feel awful.
- It is a fact that no matter what I do or say, there will always be some people who dislike me.
- It is unnecessary to justify myself to others or convince them I'm a nice person.
- Trying to win others' approval is degrading, demoralizing, and unnecessary.
- Others' approval is not worth having for its own sake.
- If I feel hurt because others think badly of me, it's because I incorrectly believe their opinion is more important than my own.
- Other people's approval is necessary only if they have something I want and they won't give it to me unless they like me.
- It's not necessary for people to like or approve of me!

- Do I become concerned when I know others think badly of me?
- Do I waste much time wondering what others think of me?
- Do I believe that being liked by others makes me a better person?
- Do I feel uncomfortable when I think people dislike me?
- Do I try to impress people or am I just myself?
- Am I concerned that people would dislike me if they found out what I was really like?
- Do I change my opinion when someone disagrees with me?
- Do I go to extremes to avoid upsetting people?
- Do I feel a need to point out my "specialness" to others?
- Do I apologize to people for things that aren't my fault?
- Do I do what I think is right, or what I think others want me to do?
- How many things do I do because of what others might think if I *didn't* do them?

# Melissa and Donna

**M**elissa works in the sales department of a large machine parts wholesaler. She had enjoyed her job until recently when her friend, Susan, quit and Donna was hired to take her place. Melissa hadn't minded sharing an office with Susan because she was a modest kind of person, much as Melissa considered herself to be. Susan's replacement, Melissa soon decided, was not.

When their supervisor introduced them, Melissa smiled and greeted the other woman, saying she hoped Donna would like working there. But her welcoming attitude changed abruptly only minutes later when she heard Donna's first sales call. Much to Melissa's surprise, it sounded as though Donna was *flirting* with her customer! The next few days confirmed Melissa's suspicions; when Donna talked with men, she considered suggestive talk her most important sales tool.

Although Melissa found the woman's conversations distasteful, at first she felt she could handle them without making a fuss. But after several weeks of listening to Donna's immodest talk, Melissa had all of it that she could stand. She had tried to tactfully express her feelings to Donna on several occasions, but each time Donna just stared at her blankly as though she didn't understand what Melissa was talking about.

Considering the circumstances, if you were Melissa, would you . . .

**1** take a class on dealing with stress?

**2** look for a job in more suitable surroundings?

**3** explain the problem to your supervisor and let her handle it?

**4** make a greater effort to ignore Donna and concentrate on your work?

**5** try again to tell Donna how bad her sales approach sounds?

**6** try to get Donna fired?

*If you chose*

**2** look for a job in more suitable surroundings, or

**6** try to get Donna fired

*You perceive the problem to be* having to contend with Donna's objectionable behavior.

*You think this is a problem because you believe* people should always behave respectably.

*You believe it can best be solved by* removing yourself from the problem or making the problem (Donna) leave you.

*PROBABLE OUTCOME:* If you decide to find another job, then with considerable inconvenience and expense to yourself, you'll find employment in a company that seems more to your liking. And you'll be happy there, too — until you are once again required to work with someone else who differs significantly from you.

If you decide to stay at your present job, you'll try to sabotage or discredit Donna in some fashion, and unless you're extremely clever, will probably be fired. In either case, it is likely you'll be on your way out the door again, taking with you the same problems with which you arrived.

*How is this likely to make you feel?* Frustrated, indignant, angry, self-pitying, and depressed. From your viewpoint, you're being forced to work under intolerable conditions.

*Will you feel good about yourself?* No. Since both of these alternatives are destined to fail in one or more ways, you'll end up feeling like an impotent victim.

*For better alternatives* see the information about Answers 1 and 4.

## LEVEL 2 ANSWERS

*If you chose*

**3** explain the problem to your supervisor and let her handle it, or

**5** try again to tell Donna how bad her sales approach sounds

*You perceive the problem to be* that Donna lacks incentive to improve her distasteful behavior.

*You think this is the problem because you believe* people will change their behavior if given good reason to.

*You believe it can best be solved by* bringing the matter to her attention or by coaxing, shaming or coercing her into behaving differently.

*PROBABLE OUTCOME:* While open and honest communication can be helpful in solving problems with others, it doesn't always work. Donna *may* be concerned when she finds she's doing something that bothers you, but then again, she may not. She would, however, have to be truly generous and accepting to not take offense at your estimation of her character, whether imparted to her by you or your supervisor. While there is a possibility your comments *won't* offend her, it's much more likely that they *will*.

Either answer would doubtless provide Donna with an incentive to do *something,* but it would probably not be the sort of response for which you were hoping. In return for your advice, Donna may tell you to mind your own business or provide you and your boss with a list of *your* traits that *she* finds offensive.

And depending on your response to *her* response, you may end up with a black eye, in a name-calling contest, or with an armed truce that makes working conditions intolerable and commissions smaller. Or, possibly, your supervisor may decide she can get along nicely without either of you, and you find that rather than solving a problem you've created some new ones.

*How is this likely to make you feel?* You may feel satisfied and justified to begin with but you will soon become unhappy, defensive, or fearful. Although you may congratulate yourself on how effectively you handled things, sooner or later you'll be unhappy and defensive when Donna inevitably demonstrates her resentment of you.

*Will you feel good about yourself?* No. Because victories of this nature are generally short-lived, you will continue to encounter this problem, whether at your current job or at another one. If Donna refuses to change, which is most likely, you'll become angry with her and with yourself, too, for failing to solve your problem. Because either battle plan is doomed to failure, you'll end up feeling victimized and inadequate.

*For better alternatives* see the information about Answers 1 and 4.

*If you chose*

**1** take a class on dealing with stress, or

**4** make a greater effort to ignore Donna and concentrate on your work?

*You perceive the problem to be* your unrealistic assumption that Donna should change her behavior to meet your expectations.

*You think this is the problem because you realize* people are unlikely to change merely because you want them to.

*You believe it can best be solved by* ignoring Donna's conversations and devoting more attention to your work.

*PROBABLE OUTCOME:* After some effort, determination, and practice, you will be able to disregard Donna's conversations. This will be to your advantage, *first*, because she will probably continue using the same conversational style as long as it works to her benefit, and *second*, because this realization will permit you to retain your personal integrity while working with people who differ from you.

*How is this likely to make you feel?* You will feel contented and pleased with yourself, not because you agree with Donna's behavior or sales techniques, but because you wisely realize that she and her sales approach are probably here to stay, so you might as well get used to them. By understanding that this problem is of your own making, you can solve it and eliminate similar problems in the future.

*Will you feel good about yourself?* Yes. Besides increasing your self-confidence and peace of mind, this solution affirms that *you* are in control in this situation and emphasizes that *you* — and not others — are in charge of your reactions.

# What's The *Real* Problem?

The real problem isn't Donna's "suggestive" sales approach, but Melissa's unrealistic belief that Donna should change and become more like her.

Melissa, to her detriment, has been playing the *"Everything Would Be Perfect If Only ..."* game. In this instance, she feels her world would be immensely improved if only Donna would behave in a manner Melissa approved of. Like the good game player she is, Melissa has not yet realized that when she has problems like this, it is generally *her* fault for creating them and not the fault of others for being the way they are.

The Melissa of Level 1 and Level 2 fails to acknowledge that *she* created this difficulty, which (in her mind, at least) relieves her of any need to change. Unfortunately, because these are non-solutions, the problem will survive intact, even if Melissa doesn't. And not only will these responses *not* work, soliciting help from Donna or her supervisor for this matter is more likely to create problems than solve them.

How does the Level 3 Melissa finally solve the problem? *First,* by replacing the unrealistic belief that Donna should change with the realistic belief that Donna has a right to work as she chooses, and *second,* by making an effort to resolve the matter within her own mind.

But what if Donna *is* actually trying to flirt with her male customers? Shouldn't Melissa inform her supervisor? Possibly, but where is the line between friendly and flirtatious, and is Melissa qualified to draw it? Since people are usually interviewed before they are hired, and presumably, Donna was, too, whoever hired her must have been comfortable with her manner. So unless her supervisor asks Melissa to spy for the company, she would be better off concentrating on improving *her* work instead of worrying about Donna's.

We can improve all our relationships considerably by understanding that it is usually wiser to respect others' differences, especially if we want them to respect *ours*. Keep these facts in mind:

1) We have no right to try to make anyone else live by our personal standards or according to our world-view.

2) When we must associate with people who are different from us, we cause unnecessary problems by making an issue of it.

3) Being different from us doesn't make anyone bad.

World peace will become reality only when humankind understands that the ways we are alike are much more important than the ways in which we are different.

# I'm Ok, But You Need Some Work

As difficult as it may be for us to believe, we continually create problems, just as Melissa did, and then blame them on others and insist they solve them! We do this with a simple, two-part technique:

**Step One:** *We decide there is something wrong with another person.* Like Melissa, we notice something about others or their behavior and label it wrong, inappropriate, or undesirable. Then we think (and often say) such things as, "She would be so much more pleasant to be around if only she didn't _______," or "I won't associate with him as long as he continues to _______," or, "They'd be so nice if only they'd stop _______."

We can make a problem out of almost anything: mannerisms, habits, attitude, or appearance. We can fabricate a problem based on how people eat or talk, on their religion, morals, or politics, or even their taste in clothing or furniture. In fact, creative individuals that we are, we can turn almost anyone's differences into a liability.

**Step Two:** *We inform the individual of the problem we've assigned to him and then tell him to correct it.* Having decided that someone differs from us in ways we consider significant, we feel justified, obligated, or possibly even *compelled* to set him straight. Certain that we speak from a loftier viewpoint, we tell him he has a problem, and often follow this announcement with a suggestion as to what he must do to make matters better. The directness with which we present this information varies, depending on how likely we are to get beaten up.

## WHY WE WANT OTHERS TO CHANGE

What motivates this curious behavior? Sometimes we fool ourselves into believing we have only the other person's welfare at heart and that we act from the most noble of motives. "I'm not asking you to change merely to please *me*," we insist, "but because it is the *right* thing for you to do.

But are our motives really so pure and admirable? Not hardly. With occasional exceptions, they are quite self-serving. In fact, if we look at ourselves honestly, we will discover we try to change others for the following reasons:

***We don't think we should have to put up with anything we don't like.*** It is amazing how many of us cling to this childish notion. This idea is left over from our nursery days when our cries and wails brought someone running to do whatever was necessary to make us feel good again. This outdated belief is the explanation for much of the irrational behavior we both see and engage in.

***We are unreasonably convinced of our correctness.*** Some of us suffer from a severe case of "Being Right." Symptoms of this affliction include being overwhelmed with our personal rightness, and being certain we know what is correct, best, or most appropriate in most circumstances for most people. We firmly believe that what seems right for us should be right for everyone. Since there are no facts to support this conclusion, instead of being the infallible source of wisdom we tell ourselves we are, we are just the victim of a limited viewpoint.

***We are trying to counter feelings of intrinsic wrongness.*** When we dislike ourselves, as too many of us do, we are eager for others to copy us. When they do, we feel accepted and validated, and consequently, feel less bad about ourselves. Our reasoning, whether done consciously or unconsciously, is, "If others choose to follow in my footsteps, I must not be so bad after all."

*We think it is easier for other people to change than it is for us.* If it occurs to us that *we* might change instead of expecting others to, we quickly dismiss the idea. Typically, we think most other people are not quite as "real" as we are; we think of them as basically two-dimensional cutouts who may indeed possess needs, desires, and hopes like we do, but certainly not with the same urgency, intensity, complexity, and importance. We think of them as being like computers, which, once they've been programmed to perform certain actions, uncomplainingly do them.

*We think we will be happier when others behave as we wish.* Because we sometimes respond to others' actions with negative emotions, we mistakenly believe their actions cause them. Consequently, we think we will be able to avoid feeling bad if we can just persuade people to alter the behavior that we believe causes it.

*We perceive others' differences as threatening.* When we try to change others because they are different from us, we expose our fears and vulnerabilities to the world. The greater our insecurity and the weaker our sense of control, the more strongly we insist that people and things fit our preconceived notions. We believe that when others act and think more like we do, they will be more predictable, and our feelings of comfort will increase.

## HOW DO OUR SUGGESTIONS AFFECT OUR RELATIONSHIPS?

Since we naively assume the wisdom of our suggestions will be immediately apparent to others once they are acquainted with them, we are dismayed to discover that most people strongly oppose our efforts to re-shape them. Instead of acknowledging our criticisms as valid, they become resentful, hurt, angry, or indignant, and correctly think of us as arrogant and insensitive. This isn't surprising, of course, because in effect, we're telling them:

- they aren't quite bright enough to figure things out for themselves

- they aren't as perceptive, intelligent, knowledgeable, or experienced as we are, or

- they standards are not as high or as acceptable as ours.

Not surprisingly, few agree with our assessment. As others see it, we want them to do the hard work of changing, so we can enjoy the benefits. To them, it is as if we are trying to dump our garbage (i.e., the problems we've created by our negative feelings about them or their behavior) on their property, instead of keeping it on our own, where it originated.

Despite vigorous protests, we are difficult to discourage. To assure those we want to remodel that our suggestions are more than mere personal preference, we try to provide legitimate-sounding reasons. We say things such as "It's for your own good," or, "It's for the best," or, "You'll thank me for this some day," or, "You'll be a better person for it," or, "Everybody else does it this way," or other equally meaningless phrases we hope will have a persuasive effect.

When we encounter resistance, instead of giving up we devise a new battle plan or try to add weight or authority to our request by insisting that morally, ethically, legally, or spiritually it is the *only* acceptable course of action. The depth of our concern for others can be measured by the amount of agony we are willing to put them through to make them as we wish them to be. If others flatly refuse to listen to our advice, we decide they are beyond help and move on to new territory.

**HOW DO OUR ATTEMPTS TO CHANGE OTHERS AFFECT US?**

Obviously, our efforts must produce effects of some sort. Unfortunately, they are rarely pleasant, either for us or for those we wish to change.

*We are unhappy a lot of the time.* Because people rightly resent and resist our attempts to change them, we are often disappointed and dissatisfied with the poor results we achieve. How deeply and how often we are disappointed is a good indicator of how far from reality our expectations have strayed.

*We fail to solve our problems.* Because we are accustomed to blaming others for our problems, we overlook the fact that we created most of them. Instead of viewing our predicaments from a helpful "What can I do about this myself?" perspective, we adopt a passive "Look what he did to me!" attitude and re-experience the problem again and again while we wait in vain for someone to fix it.

*We alienate many people.* Trying to get others to change is perhaps one of the least-applauded, least-endearing activities in which we can engage. A belief in our personal correctness, coupled with the belief that others should be willing to change to suit us tends to make us thoroughly obnoxious. Because we put people off with our superior attitude and air of authority, many respond to our efforts to "improve" them with anger, bitterness, and hostility.

*We sour or destroy our close relationships.* Too many of us believe that being involved in an intimate relationship automatically confers on us the right to remodel our partner. Few things, however, are more destructive in a romantic relationship than insisting that our partner change to meet our expectations. When we demand that others modify their behavior to suit us, we make life miserable for them, and the closer the relationship, the greater its potential for misery.

Obviously, this is not a prescription for happiness. Consequently, we must ask ourselves an extremely important question:

*If trying to persuade others to change has such ugly and unpleasant effects on everyone, why don't I stop doing it?*

## SOLVING THIS PROBLEM

Whenever you begin feeling things would be a lot better if you could just persuade someone to change their behavior in one way or another, keep these three facts in mind:

1) If we want others to honor our requests for change, we must be willing to honor theirs. Like everyone else, we are attached to our current ideas, beliefs, and behavior, and stoutly resist changing any part of them, sometimes even when it would be to our benefit. And although we may profess a willingness to entertain new and conflicting viewpoints and insist we are open to change, too often we listen to others' ideas with an open mouth and closed mind. If we want people to change their behavior, we must be willing to modify or alter *ours* if they ask us to. We cannot in good conscience ask anyone to do what we refuse to do ourselves.

2) We do not have the right to insist others be different than they are. We are not born with an innate ability to assess others' behavior objectively nor with the right to insist they change anything about them that we dislike. We become so wrapped up in our unrealistic expectations of others that we ignore the fact that most people have agendas of their own, which probably involve remaining pretty much as they are. Since there are good reasons why people are as they are, they are unlikely to change merely because we want them to. If someone *does* change at our request, we have probably received far more consideration than we deserve.

136

3) Unless people interfere with others' enjoyment of their legitimate rights, they should be free to think and do as they choose. Some of us find it extremely difficult to grasp that it is perfectly all right for others to look, think, and behave differently than we do, as long as they harm no one in the process. It is a fact of life that people will often behave in ways we consider inappropriate or unwise, and it is incredibly self-centered and naive to believe they will change their behavior just because we think they should.

What can we do to improve matters, if we find ourselves involved in the destructive business of trying to make others change? Unless someone's behavior is physically threatening, harmful, or intentionally destructive,

> *We can either change our belief about*
> *the matter or keep an open mind.*

Remember this: situations become problems only if we define them as such. Since we create many difficulties by interpreting essentially neutral circumstances or facts negatively, we can eliminate many problems merely by learning to view matters differently. Instead of saying, "This is awful!" we need to say, "Maybe it's *not* the situation that's wrong, but my ideas about it."

## THE BENEFITS OF LETTING OTHERS BE THEMSELVES

It is true that learning to view the world differently can be pretty challenging, and it's also true that it isn't the easiest thing to do. BUT, it is not just others who benefit when we decide to accept people as they are; we do, too. Letting others remain as they are will probably eliminate at least half of our daily irritations. As soon as we stop insisting people change, we'll stop frustrating ourselves when they remain the same. By allowing others a free hand with *their* lives, we remove a lot of annoyance and anger from our own. While tolerance of this kind won't compromise us in any fashion, it grants others the same freedom we want, which is to live as we see fit.

In most cases, it isn't others' behavior that is the problem, but our interpretation of it. Accepting people are happy people, because they don't create unnecessary problems by continually judging others' ideas or behavior. And because they avoid creating disapproval, they also avoid the oppressive emotional burdens that accompany it. Those of us who are the most judgmental are also the most troubled, and those who find the most faults are the most unhappy. Believing so much must change before they can be happy, they postpone happiness indefinitely.

Ultimately, it is only ourselves we can change. We can put a lot of energy into persuading people to behave as we wish, but fortunately, we lack the power to compel them. Whenever we notice ourselves feeling displeased with another person, here is something to contemplate:

> *If we were to imprison everyone who displeased another person, we would all be under lock and key.*

Think about it.

## *Important Ideas to Consider*

- Because each of us sees and interprets life from a unique perspective, values or ethics that seem admirable and reasonable to me may appear stupid, trivial, or amusing to others.
- Because my philosophy of life may seem as wrong to others as theirs seems to me, I will only waste time by wishing they were different.
- Others are as certain of the correctness of their beliefs as I am convinced of the correctness of mine.
- Situations become problems only if I choose to define them as such.
- People are not wrong or bad just because they are not like me.
- When I feel inclined to be angry with people who won't change as I wish them to, it is good to remember that I, too have not been able to change myself and become as I would like to be.
- When someone does something that bothers me but does not cause any actual harm, I should consider changing my opinion about it.
- It is at least as difficult for others to change as it is for me.
- My requests that others change may prompt reactions ranging from agreement to homicide.

## *Questions to Ask Yourself*

- Am I inclined to view others negatively if they are different from me? If so, why?
- How do I feel when someone asks me to change in some way?
- Do I have any reason to believe others don't experience the same unpleasantness and discomfort that I do when I ask them to change?
- Since I cannot be absolutely certain my ideas and beliefs are correct, do I have the right to urge anyone else to accept them?

- Do I think others should respect my desire that they change? If I do, why do I think this?

- Do I feel uncomfortable when I am with people who are different from me?

- What aspects of my life or personality might others think I should change? Should I change them?

- What would happen if I spent more time thinking about people's good points than their bad ones?

## *Experiments*

1) *Increase your understanding of others and their feelings.* Read realistic fiction and biographies of well-known individuals. Choose stories which make you imagine yourself in unfamiliar settings, as a different person who does different things (or does things differently), or as a follower of a different religion or philosophy of life.

When you talk with others, listen carefully to what they say about their feelings. Make an effort to understand why people feel as they do, and you will become aware of many new ways to look at and experience things.

2) *Become more flexible.* We are not permanently locked into our present patterns of thought and action, since the option of change is always available. Consider changing yourself in small ways. Start thinking of change as a desirable improvement. Begin looking for positive aspects to circumstances or situations you've previously thought of as negative. Make a point of deviating from your routine in at least one way, every day. Take different routes to work. Eat at new

restaurants. Meet some new people in new surroundings. Try diverse kinds of books, music, and entertainment. Begin thinking of yourself as a person who can behave differently when it is wiser and more enjoyable.

# Shana and Jason

Shana was surprised one Saturday morning when she got a call from Jason, a high school acquaintance she hadn't seen since graduation. After they had chatted for a while, Jason suggested they meet for dinner at a popular buffet restaurant and talk about old times. Since she had nothing planned for the evening, Shana agreed.

As luck would have it, they arrived at the same time and met just outside the restaurant. Once inside, they were soon shown to their table. Rather than placing her purse on their small table, Shana put it in the empty chair to her left.

She enjoyed dinner. In fact, the food was so good she even made a second trip through the buffet line. But the longer she talked with Jason, the more she realized that other than a few shared experiences from their high school days, they had extremely little in common.

Finally, after enough time had elapsed so she could leave without seeming rude, Shana told Jason she had better be going and reached for her purse. It wasn't there! She quickly checked the other vacant chair at the table and found it empty, too. Not wanting to believe the worst, she accused Jason of hiding it, for a joke, but his serious denials convinced her he hadn't. That meant her purse had been stolen!

How, Shana wondered out loud, could her bag have disappeared from the table while one or both of them were sitting there? Looking a little guilty, Jason reluctantly admitted he'd left the table for a few minutes when she returned to the buffet line.

Shana felt awful. Not only did she have credit cards in her purse, she had over $250 in cash, money she had expected to last until the end of the month. What was she going to do now?

If you were Shana, would you . . .

**1** resolve to stay away from this restaurant in the future?

**2** threaten to sue the restaurant to recover your money?

**3** realize it was a mistake to have gone out with Jason?

**4** realize you should have reminded Jason about your purse when you left the table?

**5** tell Jason it's his responsibility to repay the money you lost because of his carelessness?

**6** recognize that it was your obligation to assure the security of your belongings?

*If you chose*

**1** resolve to stay away from this restaurant in the future, or

**3** realize it was a mistake to have gone out with Jason

*You perceive the problem to be* that you were either in the wrong place or with the wrong person.

*You think this was the problem because you believe* you sometimes have bad luck.

*You believe it can best be solved by* having nothing further to do with Jason, the restaurant, or both.

*PROBABLE OUTCOME:* In the future, you'll either do without Jason's company (not a big loss), or you'll avoid the restaurant where your purse was taken (a bigger loss, since you enjoyed their food). Although either response appears to make a reccurrence of the problem less likely, they do so in regard to only one particular restaurant and one specific person. Since this kind of thinking does not foster genuine solutions, similar problems will cause you totally avoidable stress in the future.

*How is this likely to make you feel?* Disappointed, unhappy, angry, and self-pitying. You'll be angry and disappointed because you believe what happened to you isn't fair, and you'll feel unhappy and sorry for yourself because you lost money you needed badly.

*Will you feel good about yourself?* No. You will feel inadequate and helpless, knowing you've been victimized, and that there is nothing you can do about it. You may even think it's possible that bad things happen to you because you are bad yourself and deserve them.

*For better alternatives* see the information about Answers 4 and 6.



*If you chose*

**2** threaten to sue the restaurant to recover your money, or

**5** tell Jason it's his responsibility to repay the money you lost because of his carelessness

*You perceive the problem to be* getting those you believe responsible for the loss of your money to replace it.

*You think this because you believe* the theft was due to the negligence of either Jason or the restaurant.

*You believe the problem can best be solved by* convincing those you consider responsible to reimburse you.

*PROBABLE OUTCOME:* While it's not totally inconceivable that you might convince the restaurant manager or Jason to accept financial responsibility for your loss, it's extremely unlikely. What *is* likely is that both will tell you how very sorry they are and promptly disclaim any obligation or responsibility for the theft. Because neither response is likely to produce satisfactory results, you'll have to finish out the month on short rations. In addition, although you may be unaware of it, Jason will probably decide you haven't matured appreciably since high school and the restaurant manager will fervently hope you'll take your appetite and problems elsewhere.

*How is this likely to make you feel?* Worried, frustrated, angry, and resentful. You are concerned because you know you'll experience difficulties as a result of your troublesome financial situation. You will also be frustrated because of your loss and angry and resentful because others refuse to take responsibility for the damage you believe they've caused.

*Will you feel good about yourself?* No. You will feel powerless, inadequate, and insecure because your efforts have failed to improve your awkward financial condition. Since your lack of cash will be inconvenient, you'll often remind yourself throughout the month about the injustice from which you're suffering.

*For better alternatives*: see the information about Answers 4 and 6.

## LEVEL 3 ANSWERS

*If you chose*

**4** realize you should have reminded Jason about your purse when you left the table

**6** recognize that it was your obligation to assure the security of your belongings?

*You perceive the problem to be* your carelessness in allowing your purse to be stolen.

*You think this because you believe* the safety of your belongings is your own responsibility.

*You believe it can best be solved by* being more careful in the future.

*PROBABLE OUTCOME:* You'll consider the loss of your purse and money the price of your negligence. Unfortunately, this healthy attitude won't magically restore your funds or credit cards, so you'll experience some discomfort and inconvenience until your financial cloud lifts.

*How is this likely to make you feel?* Irritated, regretful, and determined. You feel irritated with yourself because you know the loss wouldn't have occurred had you been more careful. Your regret is due in equal parts to your carelessness and your upcoming hardships. Because you regard your loss as a painful and expensive (but well-learned) lesson, you are determined to prevent similar incidents in the future.

*Will you feel good about yourself?* Yes. You will accept your loss with as much grace as possible. While you don't consider having made a costly blunder something to be proud of, you have accepted responsibility for your misfortune and by doing so have greatly increased your control over your life. By understanding how *you* could have prevented the theft, you have learned how to avoid similar and possibly even greater, catastrophes in the future.

# What's the *Real* Problem?

While the central issue here seems to be the loss of Shana's purse and its contents, it is not. While losing money and credit cards is no laughing matter, that is a *secondary problem* brought about by the *primary problem*: Shana's unrealistic expectation that her purse would be safe at the table even though she had done virtually nothing to ensure that it would be.

What did she wrongly assume? Perhaps, that others would be as honest as she was, or that Jason would guard her possessions as if they were his own, or that the staff in a busy restaurant could take enough time away from their other duties to keep their eyes on the diners' belongings. But whatever she assumed, by neither taking her purse with her to the buffet line, nor mentioning it to Jason, she set herself up to be victimized.

Although the Level 1 responses may create the illusion of being able to prevent future problems, they are just a lot of smoke without fire. What has escaped Shana's notice is that her carelessness could just as easily have caused her to lose her purse in a different restaurant, with a different companion.

The Shana of Level 2 tries to shift the blame to others, a common and socially accepted means of escaping personal responsibility. If she had asked Jason or the restaurant manager for their help, and they refused to give it, she might have a legitimate complaint. And even without one, she might be able to convince Jason or the restaurant manager to accept liability for her loss if she made a great nuisance of herself, but chances are slim, because in effect, Shana is asking Jason or the manager to take responsibility for *her* mistake.

The Level 3 solutions don't solve the problem of the missing purse, but they *do* address its cause, which is Shana's unrealistic expectation that her belongings will be safe even though she does virtually nothing to *make* them safe. Unfortunately, while gaining the understanding that her expectation was unrealistic may help Shana avoid future problems, it won't restore her money or her credit cards.

# Unrealistic Expectations

Although we consider ourselves rational beings, all of us, without exception, have some baseless hopes and improbable desires polluting our minds. These ideas are inaccurate assumptions that we believe are valid. We can refer to them in a number of ways, but the term most commonly used to describe them is *unrealistic expectations.*

We don't limit them to just one or two aspects of our lives. In fact, it would not be an exaggeration to say there are few aspects of our lives about which we *do not* have some illogical hopes.

How did we arrive at these peculiar ideas? Unless we've been living on the proverbial desert island or beyond the reach of human communication, we have been exposed to them almost since our exit from the womb. Some we acquired by identifying with the highly imaginative and often fanciful ideas and behavior of characters in fiction, popular songs, games, television shows, and movies. We developed other expectations with the help of the advertising industry, which urged us to cultivate illogical yearnings for products or services that could not provide what they seemed to promise. And of course, not lacking creativity ourselves, we've concocted many fanciful ideas of our own by merging wishful thinking with an uninhibited imagination.

The absence of a factual foundation for our mental inventions doesn't bother us, though, because we think that wanting something badly enough is often sufficient reason for it to happen or appear. We excite our minds with "magical" thoughts about what we want and then expect to experience the improbable while avoiding the inevitable. Stubbornly refusing to let facts interfere with our inventiveness, we envision a future that can never arrive and live in the hope that an implausible sequence of events will miraculously take place to make our fondest wishes materialize.

## HOW UNREALISTIC EXPECTATIONS AFFECT US.

What happens when our inflated expectations are punctured by the sharp edges of reality? We experience emotional pain, ranging from mild irritation to gut-wrenching despair.

- We expect those we love to be safe from danger and death, and we react with anger and sorrow when they are badly injured or die.
- We expect others to take care of us and our interests, and we become disappointed, angry, and unhappy when we discover they have not.
- We expect someone special to enter our life and make us truly happy, but either no one does, or those who do disappoint and sadden us.
- We expect other people to think and behave much as we do, and we become disappointed, fearful, or angry when they do not.
- We expect others to live by our ethics and code of conduct, and we become angry and afraid when they do not.
- We think life should treat us fairly, and we become angry and depressed when we think it does not.
- We expect those with whom we have close relationships to know what we want without our telling them, and we become disappointed when they do not.

And what actions do we take when our hopes run counter to reality, and we are filled with intense, distressing emotions? We bitterly blame those we consider responsible for the circumstance, we become angry with God, or we go on strike against life, certain that one or all of them are responsible for our terrible pain.

This is where we make our mistake. Instead of looking outside ourselves for the source of our pain and complaining angrily or dejectedly about not getting what we expected, we should ask ourselves, "Was it reasonable for me to rely on getting this?" Or "Why is it that what I counted on to happen, didn't?" Or, "Why did that happen when I counted on it *not* to?" We should ask these questions for this reason:

> *Each emotionally painful incident we experience – no matter how big or how small — is an invitation to discover why we are hurt and what we can do to avoid similar pain in the future.*

It isn't necessary to feel like a victim. We don't *have to* suffer the destructive effects of unrealistic expectations because we have ample opportunities to revise them when we notice they're causing us pain. To accomplish this, we must make it a habit to do four things:

1) *Pay attention to emotional feedback.* It is helpful to keep in mind that *our painful emotions are the by-products of our resistance to reality.* Besides being highly unpleasant and painful, disappointment and unhappiness are clear signals that we've been living in unreality. To avoid this kind of pain in the future, think of each negative feeling as a warning sign, a flashing arrow, or screaming siren directing our attention to an unreasonable idea that is causing problems.

2) *Be receptive to new ideas and be willing to change.* It is a very human tendency to deny facts that conflict with our idealized pictures of life or our long-held, treasured beliefs. But once we have identified a problem in thinking that causes us unhappiness, we must be willing to think of that idea as the illogical assumption

that it is and replace it with an outlook based on fact and reality. If we are unwilling to acknowledge our unrealistic expectations as unrealistic, nothing else we do is likely to make any improvement.

3) ***Understand and accept that life does not treat all of us the same.*** Contrary to how it may feel at times, we have not been singled out from everyone else to experience disappointments. Many people are denied things they want or even things they desperately *need* for survival. And most people also experience *at least* one devastating tragedy during their lifetime.

It is a fact that life often distributes favors unevenly: some of us have a pretty easy time of it, and others of us don't. Once we accept that we have little or no control over certain matters in life, we can stop fighting with the world and get on with our lives.

We could spare ourselves a great deal of suffering if, instead of being so demanding of life, we maintained an openness to whatever comes. While it is fine to *want* certain things to happen, we must acknowledge that they may never occur. Mental flexibility is important in this regard, as is *letting* things happen instead of *insisting* they do. Sometimes it is best to let go and have *no* expectations. When we learn to prefer instead of insisting, and we are less rigid about what we expect from the future, we will discover and enjoy many unexpected pleasures.

- I can eliminate a lot of stress and frustration by giving life the freedom to unfold as it must, not as I insist..
- If I am observant and thoughtful I will learn much about the accuracy of my assumptions.
- Resisting what happens is futile, but learning from it is good.
- It is okay for me to prefer things be a certain way, but not to demand that they be.
- Whenever I am unhappy, it is because I have expected too much or too unrealistically.
- My negative emotions are the by-products of my resistance to reality.
- If things turn out differently than I expect, it is not the situation that is at fault, but my expectations.
- It would be wonderful if just desiring something would make it happen, but that isn't how life works.
- Things do not happen merely because I want them to, they happen for reasons.
- Rather than having expectations of others, let them reveal themselves to you.
- When I am disappointed, the problem is not that God, life, or other people have failed me, but that I have been asking more than I can reasonably expect to get.
- Unrealistic expectations produce disappointment and anger.

## *Questions to Ask Yourself*

- Do I often feel disappointed?
- How wise is it for me to resist reality?

- How often each day do I experience unpleasant feelings as a result of my unrealistic expectations?
- Why do I continue to have the same expectations when they fail to materialize?
- Do I believe life owes me certain things?

## *Experiments*

1) Think about an incident that happened recently, to which you responded with anger or disappointment.

- What turned out differently than you expected?
- What did you expect to happen?
- How did you feel?
- Since what you expected didn't happen, how must you change your expectations about this kind of situation if it occurs in the future?
- If other people were involved in this incident, were they aware of what kind of behavior you expected from them?

Do this exercise at least once each day for a month. Write down each unreasonable assumption you uncover. If you keep a diary of these, and consult it often, you will be amazed at how different life will look.

2) Listen carefully to what you and other people say and identify specific patterns of speech that indicate too much reliance on unreality, such as

> "I hope..."
> "I wish..."
> "If only he/she/it would..."

"He/she should have...."

"She/he shouldn't have....."

"Why didn't you do what I expected?"

"It's not fair!"

"Why do these things always happen to me?"

When you hear one of these expressions, whether spoken by you or by someone else, you can expect it to be followed by an unrealistic expectation. Make a point of removing these phrases (and their accompanying expectations) from your habitual speech.

CHAPTER 10
# Connie and the Solicitors

**A**s Connie drove to a nearby discount store late one Saturday morning, she savored the unseasonably warm weather and enjoyed the brilliant fall colors dominating the landscape. She wished she could spend the next hour cleaning out her flowerbeds, but she knew she would be in the discount store for some time. Her schedule had been so full recently that she'd had to put off buying many things she needed and, as a result, had compiled quite a lengthy shopping list.

Arriving at the store, Connie's eyes scanned the parking lot, searching for an empty space near the door. As she did, she glanced toward the store's entrance and noticed several people standing there. Two of them were wearing brightly colored vests and holding what she assumed must be cans for collecting donations, since people appeared to be putting something into them. As she drove closer to the door, one of the collectors smiled and waved to her. With a sinking heart, Connie waved back as she recognized the wife of one of her close business associates.

While Connie made generous donations to a number of charities each year, they were causes she had selected because they held a special significance for her. From her viewpoint, it was one thing to contribute to a cause she knew to be worthwhile, but quite another to be aggressively solicited to support one about which she knew little or nothing.

As far as she was concerned, having to pass by the solicitors in order to do her shopping was like running the gauntlet. Glumly, she wondered what to do.

If you were in Connie's place would you be more likely to . . .

**1** say, "I already gave," even though you hadn't?

**2** tell them, "No, thank you," because you didn't want to give to their charity?

**3** come back tomorrow or go to a different store?

**4** make a small donation **on** your way in?

**5** make a small donation **and** complain to the manager after you got inside?

**6** greet the solicitors **as you** enter the store, even though you don't donate?

*If you chose*

**3** come back tomorrow or go to a different store, or

**4** make a small donation on your way in

*You perceive the problem to be* avoiding feelings of guilt.

*You think this is a problem because you believe* you are obligated to help whenever you are asked, no matter how awkward or inconvenient for you.

*You believe it can best be solved by* avoiding the solicitors entirely or donating just a small amount.

*PROBABLE OUTCOME:* If you postpone your shopping until tomorrow or go to another store, you'll put yourself to a lot of inconvenience. Besides this, there is no guarantee that you won't encounter solicitors at other stores, whether you shop today or tomorrow.

If you give in and make a donation, you will do so grudgingly, with a feeling of irritation and resentment, instead of the pleasure you ordinarily feel when you make donations to your favorite charities. Since both Level 1 responses sidestep the main problem, they perpetuate it, rather than solve it.

*How is this likely to make you feel?* Annoyed, resentful, and guilty. You resent being put in a position where, instead of being able to shop as you intended, you must choose between two undesirable options to avoid feeling guilty. To make things worse, those of us who believe we *must* give when we are asked generally feel guilty when we don't, no matter how we've managed to avoid it.

*Will you feel good about yourself?* No. You will feel victimized ("Why does this kind of thing always happen to me?") and manipulated because the situation seems outside your control. Either answer will intensify any feelings of weakness you now have. You may make yourself feel even *more* inadequate by thinking that if you were only richer or smarter, you could avoid this kind of situation.

*For better alternatives* see the information about Answers 2 and 6.

## LEVEL 2 ANSWERS

*If you chose*

**1** say, "I already gave," even though you hadn't, or

**5** make a small donation and complain to the manager after you got inside

*You perceive the problem to be* avoiding others' negative judgments.

*You think this is a problem because you believe* it's important that most people have a good opinion of you.

*You believe it can best be solved by* convincing those collecting money that you've already given to their cause or by persuading the store manager to not allow charities to use their premises for fund-raising.

*PROBABLE OUTCOME:* The success of the Level 2 Answers depends on how persuasive (or how good a liar) you are. You might be able to convince those collecting money that you've already made a donation, but they, like you, probably believe most people who say that aren't telling the truth. While it's not inconceivable that the store manager may agree with you, it is unlikely because many stores are under pressure from charitable organizations to permit these activities. But, even if he or she agrees to your request, it is only *this* store that will be affected, so you'll undoubtedly run into the same problem at other businesses.

*How is this likely to make you feel?* Guilty, embarrassed, resentful, indignant, and angry. You will feel guilty if you lie to the charity volunteers and uncomfortable and embarrassed if you talk to the manager. But regardless of your Level 2 answer, you will feel indignant, angry, and resentful because you feel you've been put in a position where you must either make a donation, or pretend that you have, to avoid looking like a cheapskate. In addition, you will probably feel angry because you've assured yourself that no one has the right to put you in a position where your charitable giving (or lack of it) may become public knowledge.

*Will you feel good about yourself?* No. You'll feel victimized and inadequate because you didn't solve the problem satisfactorily. To make matters worse, each time you are confronted by this kind of situation in the future (and there will be many of them) you'll re-experience the same unpleasant emotions you're feeling now.

*For better alternatives* see the information about Answers 2 and 6.



**LEVEL 3 ANSWERS**

*If you chose*

**2** tell them, "No, thank you," because you didn't want to give to their charity, or

**6** greet them in a friendly manner as you enter the store, even though you don't donate

*You realize there is no problem* unless you create one by being unrealistically concerned about what people think of you.

*You think this because you believe* your own opinion of yourself is the most important.

*PROBABLE OUTCOME:* You will go into the store, complete your shopping, and leave when you are finished, without causing yourself mental or emotional distress.

*How is this likely to make you feel?* Comfortable. Because you've accomplished the shopping you set out to do without compromising your integrity, self-respect, or self-esteem.

*Will you feel good about yourself?* Yes, because you've not done anything to feel bad about.

# What's the *Real* Problem?

The real question facing Connie is this: should she allow her moods and actions to be dictated by a concern for others' opinions?

The Level 1 responses ignore this issue and focus instead on how best to avoid the feelings of guilt she'll inflict on herself if she fails to make the donation she feels is expected. Instead of trying to avoid this unnecessary, self-imposed guilt, she could spend her time more profitably wondering if guilt is an appropriate emotion to experience under these circumstances.

The Connie of Level 2 believes that, in general, others' opinions of her are more important than her own. Because she's excessively concerned about the solicitors' approval, she reasons "These people are collecting money for what they consider a good cause. If I don't make a contribution, or at least *say* I've made one, they'll think I'm too poor or too cheap."

But will they? Might they not instead wish they were as strong as she is and envy her the self-confidence and independence that allows her to pass by the donation cans without concern for their opinions? Or might the solicitors, because they are unconcerned about others' opinions themselves, never even give the matter a thought?

When Connie chose a Level 3 solution, she did so because she has ranked concern for others' approval near the bottom of her priority list. She understands that making a donation because she feels pressured to is a poor reason for parting with even a tiny amount of cash. She is aware, too, that there are times when she must risk disapproval if she is to feel good about herself.

# Beliefs

What caused Connie's problems in the preceding scenario? The culprits were some incorrect ideas she believed were true. She created the Level 1 problem because she believed she must always provide help when she was asked. She created the Level 2 problem because she believed others' opinions of her were more important than her own.

There was no problem at Level 3, however, because the Connie of that Level *knows from practical experience* that under most circumstances her own opinion of herself is the most important. The difference between the Connie of Levels 1 and 2 and the Connie of Level 3 is that she *avoided* creating a problem by relying on a *fact* instead of a belief.

## THE THREE KINDS OF IDEAS THAT MOTIVATE US

Appearances to the contrary, we humans generally do not engage in random behavior. When we perform an action, it is because we are motivated to act by one or more ideas. What kind of ideas motivate us? There are three kinds: *facts, beliefs, and reasonable assumptions.*

### Facts

A *fact* is an idea that we *know* is true because we've seen evidence that it is, or we've verified it through personal experience. For instance, we consider the following statements facts because we know they are true:

- I will get burned if my skin comes in contact with something extremely hot.
- Gravity causes water to flow downhill.
- Sharp objects can cut me.
- A human being needs oxygen to remain alive.

Obviously, since facts are true, it is smartest to act as though they are. Ignoring the fact that we need oxygen to live or that a knife can cut us may prove dangerous or even fatal. Since facts are based on reality, when we refer to a fact, we say "I know."

## Beliefs

A *belief* is an idea that we substitute for a fact or a reasonable assumption. Lacking facts about matters we consider important, we turn to our imagination to help us determine *a)* what *might* be true, *b)* what is *likely* to be true, *c)* what we *want* to be true, or *d)*, what we are *afraid* is true. A belief, we might say, is the closest thing to the truth that we can imagine.

Here are some common beliefs:

- My emotional responses are caused by what happens to me.
- Some races and ethnic groups are inherently superior.
- Men are more intelligent than women.
- People who behave differently than I do are bad.

Because beliefs are subjective (personal) and can't be proved, they should be prefaced with the qualifiers, "I think" or "I believe."

## Reasonable Assumptions

A *reasonable assumption* consists of both belief and fact. When we have *some* facts but not enough to make a decision, we blend what we *know* is true with what we *think* may be true and create a reasonable assumption. The following are reasonable assumptions:

- The sun will rise tomorrow.
- There will always be a war going on somewhere on earth.
- The cost of living will continue to increase.
- There will always be dishonest politicians.

How reasonable our assumptions are, of course, depends on the ratio of facts to guesswork.

Since reasonable assumptions are made up of both imagined and factual ideas and can often be partly proved, when we refer to them we usually say "probably," "maybe," "usually," or "generally."

## YOU ARE WHAT YOU BELIEVE

If what we believed had no tangible effect on us or others, it would make little difference how much nonsense we've tucked away in our heads. But this isn't the case. What we believe is vitally important because beliefs can motivate us as strongly as facts.

Keep this fact in mind:

> **No matter how false, destructive, or irrational**
> **an idea might be, if we genuinely believe it,**
> **we treat it as a fact and act as though it's true.**

How do our beliefs affect us? There is an ancient tale from India that tells of a man who, while walking home after dark, came upon an object he assumed was a snake coiled on the path in front of him. Believing it *was* a snake, he proceeded to beat it with a piece of wood until he had "killed" it, only to find out the next morning that he had been beating a coiled-up rope.

Does this story have a a message for us? Yes, and a very clear one; if we act on beliefs instead of facts, we may behave foolishly, irrationally, and destructively and engage in some pretty bizarre activities.

## WHAT CAN HAPPEN WHEN
## WE ACT ON INCORRECT BELIEFS?

*Inaccurate beliefs can create chaos in our lives.* When we act on something we *know* is true, our actions work to our advantage. When we act on ideas with little or no foundation in fact, the results of our actions may be nonsensical or harmful instead of beneficial.

Think about the preceding scenarios. Whether the central characters actually created a problem or just had the opportunity to, *all* the potential or actual problems were caused by someone acting on incorrect beliefs.

- Stan had a problem because he had believed his wife's happiness was more important than his own. (Chapter 2)
- Carla created a problem if she believed Joan's needs were more important than her own. (Chapter 3)
- Karen created a problem if she believed others must approve of her appearance. (Chapter 4)
- Brian and Sally created a problem by believing they could always rely on others' goodwill and generosity. (Chapter 5)
- Richard created a problem by believing his father had a right to choose Richard's career. (Chapter 6)
- Mikki created a problem if she believed Paul's opinion of her was important. (Chapter 7)
- Melissa created a problem by believing it was Donna's obligation to change. (Chapter 8)
- Shana created a problem by believing Jason would safeguard her property in her absence. (Chapter 9)
- Connie created problems if she believed others' approval was more important than her own. (Chapter 10)

*Inaccurate beliefs limit our happiness.* How happy are you? You are as happy as you believe you have a right to be. If you enjoy life and have rewarding relationships, it is because you believe you deserve to have them. If, on the other hand, life seems unpleasant and your relationships unsatisfactory, it is not because that is how it *must* be but because that is how you consciously or unconsciously believe it *should* be. Speaking generally, what occurs to us externally usually occurs first inside our head.

*Inaccurate beliefs can be dangerous*. By itself, an incorrect belief may cause little damage. But beliefs work together like the chemicals in a formula or the ingredients in a recipe. Some mistaken ideas that are relatively harmless in themselves can provoke violence and destruction when combined with others. Here are a few examples:

- If we overlay the belief that the opposite sex is no good with the belief that it's important to be married, we will attract unpleasant partners and have unhappy relationships and ugly divorces.

- If we combine the belief that it is appropriate to dislike those who are different from us with the conviction that we shouldn't have to put up with things we dislike, we may react to others' differences with anything from avoidance to homicide.

- If we believe we're entitled to have whatever we want and also believe others' rights are less important than our own, we will try to satisfy our desires by taking advantage of people and, in doing so, are likely to lose our friends, freedom, or life.

- If we believe we have little worth as a person and also believe only worthwhile people deserve the good things in life, we will have a joyless, uncomfortable, and unpleasant existence.

Obviously, then, if we are to avoid acting illogically and making a mess of things, our beliefs must be as accurate as possible. And since the accuracy of a belief depends greatly on the reliability of its source, we must be certain our sources are credible. Unfortunately, credibility *is* the problem because we've acquired much of what we believe from two highly unreliable sources: ourselves and others.

## THE SOURCES OF OUR INCORRECT BELIEFS

### We Misled Ourselves

During the process of growing up, we reached conclusions, formulated opinions, and acquired many of our rules for living. Regrettably, we were ill-prepared for these important tasks. Because we were short on experience, knowledge, logic, and sophistication and were not yet able to compare and evaluate ideas, we developed a substantial number of inaccurate beliefs we still cling to today.

We developed some beliefs through observing others' behavior. When we saw that someone's actions appeared to produce the results he or she desired, we drew conclusions about what was or wasn't useful or appropriate conduct. Because of our inexperience, however, we didn't realize that *a)* the behavior on which we based our judgments was at times objectionable, ineffective, or unrealistic, and *b)* while this was one possible way to handle a certain kind of situation, there were many options available.

When uncertainty about a particular issue caused us discomfort and we were short on facts, rather than reserving our judgment, we upgraded our best guess to the status of a belief. Doubtless, the assumptions we made seemed appropriate at the time, but that was only because we were as yet unaware of the larger world.

And because we were inexperienced and immature, we didn't understand that wide acceptance of a particular belief meant only that it was widely accepted. So, when we found that most people seemed to believe a specific thing, we decided to believe it, too. We were like Robert Funk in *Honest to Jesus,* who confesses, "...in the exuberance of youth, I thought it extremely important to hold the correct opinions.

I didn't really know what the correct opinions were, but friends and others around me seemed to know, so I embraced theirs when I could understand them and sometimes when I couldn't."

## We Were Misled by Others

We can't take all the credit for misinforming ourselves, of course, because like infectious diseases, beliefs spread easily from one person to another. From babyhood onward, we have been surrounded by people only too eager to stuff our heads with their personal (but not necessarily accurate) visions of reality, and stuff it they did.

We've absorbed beliefs from the authority figures who guided and trained us. This category includes almost anyone we respected, liked, or had reason to obey, but especially our parents and teachers. Many of us underwent some form of religious training, which consisted primarily of being told to believe a great many things for which we were given little or no proof.

In addition to these sources of misinformation, we've immersed ourselves in doubtful ideas issuing from the media, via television, motion pictures, novels, and popular songs. They have provided us with unrealistic ideas about life, love, and marriage, and about the acceptability of violent behavior.

Advertising professionals have sought to instill in us beliefs that will increase their clients' profitability, teaching us that we should be tanned, slender, beautiful or handsome, and in general, more desirable. They have also taught us that not only do we need to improve how we look, we must acquire any number of attributes and qualities which we will have only if we use their client's products. They seek to channel our thoughts away from the reality around us to a reality they've created.

Why did we accept so much unverified information as fact? Here are some of the reasons.

- As children, we were extremely uncritical and incorrectly assumed that those who were older or more self-assured were also wiser and more knowledgeable.
- The possibility that certain beliefs are true is so pleasing to us that we insist they *must* be true.
- Because we wanted to be accepted by certain groups and feel that we "belonged," we adopted whatever beliefs were necessary to make us acceptable to them.
- At times we accepted what people told us only because we wanted to please them.
- Some of us found it better to say we *did* believe dubious or illogical ideas because saying we didn't meant getting unwelcome attention, or being punished or left out.
- Because we had great respect for some people and considered them trustworthy, it never occurred to us to doubt anything they said.
- We accepted religious beliefs only because we were told that *not* accepting them would result in dire consequences.

Unfortunately, even after we became adults and were free to examine the validity of our beliefs, few of us did. Because we are typically encouraged to believe rather than investigate, it didn't occur to us to review the ideas we'd absorbed to verify their accuracy or appropriateness. As a result, most of the beliefs we've acquired remain in our subconscious, obeyed and unchallenged unless we are confronted with information that proves conclusively that they are false.

Not everything others taught us was faulty, of course, nor were all the conclusions we reached independently in error. In fact, we have absorbed a great many sound, sensible, and ultimately beneficial ideas over our lifetime. The trouble is, *these* ideas exist side by side with flawed and utterly false ideas masquerading as facts. And not surprisingly, because our actions can be inspired by either truth or fiction, at times we behave rationally and at other times we do not.

What's the solution to this problem? There's only one real answer.

## CHANGING OUR MIND

Obviously, if faulty ideas can produce problems, it is essential that our beliefs be as close as possible to the truth. So we must each ask ourselves, "How much of what I believe isn't true? And which of my problems are due to my incorrect beliefs?" We may flatter ourselves that we've been too clever to be taken in by any questionable or false beliefs, but this is merely another of our false beliefs.

How can we tell if something we believe is causing problems? Here are three common symptoms:

1) *We experience unpleasant emotions*, some of which may be severe. Most commonly we'll feel unhappy, disappointed, lonely, embarrassed, frustrated, or angry.

2) *We have many problems with others.* Do we look forward to spending time with other people or do we prefer to remain at a distance? Do we get along well with friends, relatives, and co-workers or do we exist in a state of armed truce? Do we feel most people are decent human beings or do they seem hostile, unfriendly, antagonistic, ignorant, or stupid?

3) *We have a poor opinion of ourselves.* Do we think we're a pretty decent human being most of the time? Can we genuinely forgive ourselves when we've done something wrong or do we go on punishing ourselves indefinitely? Do we believe we deserve the best life has to offer or feel we must settle for something less?

How many of these problems sound familiar?

## WE ARE RELUCTANT TO CHANGE

Since acting on incorrect ideas can cause any number of difficulties, shouldn't we, as intelligent, reasoning individuals, leap at the chance to correct or replace any beliefs that cause us harm? Of course we should. But the truth is that even though some of our beliefs may cause horrendous problems, they feel "right" to us. This is not necessarily because they *are* true but because *any* idea we've held for some time seems true to us, *even if it's totally false.*

Some of us feel threatened and insecure when we contemplate change because we're afraid that tampering with our beliefs will somehow alter the essential "us," and we will lose part or all of our "real" self. This fear is absolutely groundless. Shedding unrealistic ideas will neither cost us our individuality nor turn us into an emotionally shapeless blob. Beliefs are like clothing, and no matter what we put on or take off and regardless of how the details differ from time to time, at the center we are still the same. Rather than leaving us psychologically impaired or deprived, shedding inaccurate beliefs aligns our lives more closely with reality, making us feel happier, more complete, and more "real" than we've ever been.

Even though the idea of modifying our belief system may seem forbidding, it's actually a familiar process because knowingly or unknowingly, we modify our beliefs continually as we encounter new ideas, new people, and new experiences. Are we the same person we were when we were ten years old, or when we were twenty, or thirty, or forty? Our belief system is not a rigid, unalterable structure but a fluid framework of ideas that grows and evolves as we continue to learn more about the world around us. Consider the investigation of your beliefs a matter of updating your belief system.

**WHAT DO WE DO NOW?**

Perhaps the most valuable course of study any educational institution could offer would be one that encouraged people to re-evaluate their existing beliefs. In such a class we would carefully review our major premises, check them for accuracy, assess their positive or negative effects, and then make rational decisions regarding keeping, altering, or discarding them.

Since this eminently sensible program has not yet found its way onto any school's curriculum, we must each perform an investigation of our own. Let us begin boldly by establishing this as our most important ground rule:

> **No matter how long we've believed it, who else believes it, or where it came from initially, no belief is too sacred to escape our critical examination.**

We must be ruthless as we examine our beliefs and be prepared to renounce any idea, no matter how hallowed by time or tradition, and regardless of how much we love, respect, or fear those who imparted it to us. If our careful scrutiny leads us to believe an idea is untrue or unsupportable, or we can't find a valid reason to cling to it, let us, instead of believing it, reserve our judgment and maintain a "wait and see" attitude.

It's not necessary to re-evaluate every belief we have, of course. Besides being an incredibly tedious and time-consuming project, many matters are simply not significant enough to warrant an in-depth examination. It is our *major* beliefs we must investigate: those relating to values, love, morals, religion, sex, relationships, and especially, ourselves. Since our ideas about these subjects can as easily produce great pain as great happiness, they deserve our most thorough, objective examination.

Here are some rules and guidelines you'll find helpful in changing your mind:

- Remember, *you don't have to have a belief or opinion about everything!* Think of yourself as a student of life with an open, inquiring mind and a desire for wisdom. When you don't know for sure whether something is or is not a fact, just keep an open mind until you see proof that it is one or the other.

- *Ask for proof.* No matter how vigorously people insist that what they believe is correct, it can be unwise to rely on anyone's judgment but your own. While listening to and considering people's ideas can be helpful, when someone claims a particular thing is true, it's your right to ask him for evidence. If he cannot provide you with some, you have no reason to believe him.

- *Be willing to experiment.* Give honest consideration to ideas that conflict with your present ones. If you don't, you may unknowingly discard some that are more accurate and would serve you better than your current beliefs. When you encounter an opposing opinion, ask yourself, "What would happen if I believed *this* idea instead of what I believe now? Would it make things better or worse? Would *I* feel better or worse?" Instead of saying, "No," to a new idea, say, "I'll give it some thought," or "I'd like to think more about this," or "I'll give it a try."

- *Be conscious of your own fallibility.* When you are tempted to make yourself or anyone else miserable because of something you *believe* but don't *know*, remember that you are as likely to be wrong as right. No matter how much you assure yourself that *your* beliefs about a particular matter are the right ones, some individuals who are as smart or smarter than you will strongly disagree.

- *Make it a habit to distinguish beliefs from facts.* Whenever you are presented with new information which, if true, has the potential to affect your life, verify its accuracy before accepting it as a fact. If this is impossible, keep in mind that it is best to act cautiously on unverified information.

- *Choose the belief that offers the greatest benefit.* When it is impossible to determine the truth about a particular matter, but you must have a belief on which to base your actions, select the belief that promotes the greatest harmony, happiness, and peace for everyone involved. Why accept an unverifiable belief which will make you or others unhappy when there are better options available?

- *Remember that beliefs are a matter of choice.* Before you began to act as though a particular idea was factual, you first had to decide that it was, even if you made that decision unconsciously. Since you are always free to make a different decision, you are not compelled to adhere to your original choice.

- *Don't automatically accept the word of experts or authorities.* No matter how revered, respected, or honored they may be, not all those who are supposed to know what they're talking about actually do. Many times people merely parrot what they have been told by others. And because research and study provide new information with ever-increasing rapidity, today's "expert opinion" may be the basis for tomorrow's malpractice suit.

## WHERE DOES IT ALL END?

It is impossible to avoid acting on beliefs at times because in the absence of facts, we must have *some* ideas or premises on which to base our actions and structure our lives. But if we wish to be on better terms with ourselves and the rest of the world, it is essential we do three things:

1) become aware of the beliefs which motivate us
2) review them for accuracy and
3) open our minds to receive, explore, and (sometimes) accept new ideas.

Investigating and evaluating our beliefs may not be easy, and we may resist doing it, especially if we think we already know the answers to most of life's important questions. But if we *do* investigate what we believe and evaluate it with our mature judgment, we'll arrive at truly workable solutions, based not on erroneous ideas but on *our own* experience. And because we will have developed these ideas for ourselves, they will be more appropriate for us than any other beliefs could be.

How much of what we believe to be true actually *is?* How often in the course of our day do we base our actions on faulty information that produces discord and difficulties? How many of our current problems exist because we believe things that aren't true? These are all important questions, but perhaps the most important one is this: Do I actually want to go on believing things that aren't true since there's a fifty-fifty chance I'll behave irrationally, foolishly, or harmfully? Do I want to be a "loose cannon" that may explode anytime, anyplace, and for almost any reason?

Since we humans can be flexible when we choose to be, the question is not, *can* we investigate and change the beliefs which work against us, but *will* we? If you choose to *not* examine the premises on which you base your behavior, you will remain a prisoner of your mental and emotional conditioning. But if you choose to grow and develop as a person, then your mind and the beliefs and ideas which that pervade it must grow and develop, too.

Ultimately, it amounts to this: We can think, or we can believe, and the more we do of one, the less we will do of the other. And to the extent that we rely on beliefs rather than facts to sustain us, we exchange the world of reality for a fantasy world in our mind.

## *Important Ideas to Consider*

- Due to limitations of experience, education, and insight, *everyone* believes things which are untrue.
- There are no universally accepted standards of right and wrong or good and bad.
- When I am prejudiced, I see only what I think I'll see.
- If I had been raised in a different culture or religion, I might think much of what I believe now to be ridiculous or laughable.
- The more different a belief is from mine, the more I am likely to consider it strange, weird, and wrong.
- Unless I subject them to verification, I should avoid accepting the values and beliefs of unhappy people.
- When we teach children our own rules for living, we call it "instilling values." When children are taught rules different from ours, we call it "brainwashing."

- Some of the things I believe are incorrect or untrue.
- My ideas about life are based more on my *interpretation* of events than on the events themselves.
- There is no "right" or "correct" viewpoint, there are only viewpoints.
- All beliefs, without exception, should be open to question.
- One of the weakest reasons to believe something is that many other people believe it.
- Only when I give up all beliefs am I free to be who I am.

## *Questions to Ask Yourself*

- If I avoid doing harm intentionally, help those who are unable to help themselves, and respect others' rights as much as I do my own, what other rules do I need to guide me?
- When I am asked why I think a particular belief is true, do I ever respond by saying things such as "Because it's true," or "I just believe it, that's all," rather than supplying a valid reason? If I do this, what am I trying to hide?
- Which of my beliefs would seem strange to people of a different religion or from a different culture?
- Did the people from whom I learned my most important beliefs know what they were talking about?
- Where am I on the continuum between the unquestioning acceptance of the immature and the questioning attitude of the mentally mature?
- How much of my behavior is patterned after that of people I dislike, who nonetheless seemed to accomplish their objectives by using it?
- Are my opinions actually mine, or have I acquired them from others?

- How much of my behavior is based on beliefs I am not certain are true?
- Does my believing one thing and others believing another ever cause problems?
- How many things do I believe only because I've been told I should?

## *Experiments*

1) Our beliefs about certain aspects of life have a profound effect on us and those with whom we come in contact. Some of these important areas are:

> 1) sex
>
> 2) religion
>
> 3) relationships
>
> 4) ourselves
>
> 5) love
>
> 6) ethics and ideas about right and wrong
>
> 7) other people

Apply the following questions to each item on the list and ask yourself these questions:

- Who or what was the main source of my information about _______?
- Did I acquire my beliefs about _______ by reasoning things out for myself, through personal experience, or by accepting what others told me to believe?
- If I learned my beliefs about _______ from others, did they acquire them from people who had first-hand experience?
- How old was I when I acquired my beliefs about _______? Was I mature enough to evaluate them at that time?

- Were the persons from whom I learned about _________ever mistaken?
- Could their ideas about _________ have been wrong, too?
- Did their beliefs about _________ make their lives any happier?
- How do my beliefs about _________ affect me?
- Do they make me and others, if not happier, then at least not *un*happy?
- Do they make me feel good about myself?
- Do they make me behave in a friendly manner?
- Do they make me a pleasant person to be around?
- Do they encourage me to have positive feelings about most other people?
- Do my beliefs about _________ have a positive effect on my life?
- Do others have different beliefs about _________ than I do?
- Is there any evidence to support these opposing arguments?
- Is there any real evidence that what I believe about _________ is true? And if there isn't, why do I believe it?

Now go back to the top and begin asking these same questions about the next item on the list.

2) Think of something unpleasant that happened to you recently.

- Which of your beliefs makes you feel bad about this incident?
- Do you think you have no choice but to respond to this kind of situation with emotional pain?
- How would you feel about this situation if you believed differently?
- How would your life be different if you changed some of your beliefs about this kind of incident?

- What ideas would you have to change to avoid this pain in the future?

3) When you notice you're experiencing emotional pain, ask yourself what you believe that makes these circumstances seem painful? When you've discovered which belief(s) are influencing your feelings, consider revising your thinking about them. You can eliminate many problems by simply changing your ideas or beliefs about them. When you do, you solve your problems inside your head, where most of them were created. Keep in mind that problems you solve internally generally remain solved, while those you try to solve externally, don't. Although changing your viewpoint to resolve a problem may seem weak or lacking in character, it is just the opposite. When you internalize a problem, you change it from something you *can't* solve to something you *can*.

4) Stop being so sure about things. Reserve some of your brain cells for open-mindedness. Be prepared to question any or all of your ideas, including those you've believed for years. Practice saying the phrases, "I don't know," "I haven't decided yet," or "I'm going to wait and see," until you feel comfortable with them. Some people go through their entire life believing things that are not only incorrect, but foolish. Don't be one of them.

## The Seven Worst Reasons to Believe Anything

1) "Someone I trust, admire, like, respect, or am afraid of told me it was true." (Did he or she speak from personal experience or just from hearsay?)

2) "My family has always believed this." (This form of ancestor-worship is as unnecessary as it is unrealistic, besides leaving us open to all kinds of foolishness.)

3) "I was told it was true by a well-known authority." (How long will this information be true? Do other authorities agree one hundred percent with this authority? Medical discoveries, for instance, go out of date quickly as new research supercedes them.)

4) "I was told I would suffer terribly if I didn't believe certain things." (Is there any evidence this is true? Have you talked with others who have suffered as you have been told you would? Have you talked with people who didn't believe these things, but who didn't seem to be particularly unhappy? )

5) "Everybody else believes it." (That is quite literally impossible; there is *nothing* that absolutely everyone believes.)

6) "All my friends think it is true." (See No. 1, above.)

7) "I read it in a magazine or a book, or I saw it on television or the Internet, or I heard it on the radio." (Many people assume that statements made on or in these media must be accurate. In fact, each of them regularly misinform us.)

# CHAPTER 11

# Joe and the Team

Anyone who knows Joe also knows he is a baseball enthusiast. Besides watching every major league game on television, he and a group of other young people play baseball on week nights and compete with other area teams on weekends.

Neither Joe nor his teammates are professionals, but they still win most of their games and last year even made it to the state amateur league playoffs. But whether they win or lose, after each game the team visits a pizza parlor, to enjoy pizza and beer, of course, but mainly to talk over the game.

That's when Joe's problems start. After a few mugs of beer, he sometimes becomes loud and boisterous. In fact, as a result of his unruly behavior, about a month ago the team was asked to leave a restaurant and was given firm instructions not to return. Last Saturday at a different restaurant, Joe once again celebrated too enthusiastically and the manager told the team to not only quiet down or leave, but to find some other place for its future parties. As a result, the team planned to go to a different pizza parlor after the next game.

Although Saturday's game got off to a slow start, by the end of the ninth inning, Joe was jubilant; the score was eleven to two in their favor. As the team members gathered their equipment prior to leaving the field, Joe overheard some negative comments about him and his actions at the pizza parlor on the previous Saturday, and his spirits abruptly fell. When Tom, the catcher, asked Joe if he was coming along with the team, Joe didn't know what to say. Although he didn't think he had behaved that badly, it was clear that some of his teammates saw things differently.

Under the circumstances, if you were Joe, would you think it best to . . .

**1** go with the team but ask some of your teammates to tell you if you get out of line?

**2** tell Tom you've made other plans and then go home?

**3** think the restaurant managers were unnecessarily harsh?

**4** quit the team because you were angry about the comments you'd heard?

**5** ask the bartender to stop serving you if you start to get loud?

**6** go along with the team, and drink only soft drinks?

*If you chose*

**3** think the restaurant managers were unnecessarily harsh, or

**4** quit the team because you were angry about the comments you'd heard

*You perceive the problem to be* that people are overreacting to your conduct.

*You think this because you believe* no one should object just because you're having a little fun.

*You believe it can best be solved by* avoiding either the team or the restaurants where you're unwelcome.

*PROBABLE OUTCOME:* You will be excluded from the post-game celebrations, quit the team, or both. And no matter how good a pitcher you are, most of your teammates will probably be glad to see the last of you. While they may win fewer games without your pitching skills, their disappointment will be offset substantially by the more congenial after-game get-togethers..

Because of your love for baseball, you will probably join a different team and strike out with them, too, when they discover what your current teammates have already learned. At this point, you will either become wiser and work on eliminating the *real* problem, or you'll move on to yet another team.

*How is this likely to make you feel?* Hurt, angry, indignant, and misunderstood. Despite your trying to shift the blame to the restaurant managers or your fellow players, your teammates' comments will bother you and you'll wonder how much truth there is to them. You will feel unappreciated and misjudged by everyone because, as you see it, you were just trying to have a good time.

***Will you feel good about yourself?*** No. You'll feel inadequate, unacceptable, and rejected, and because you believe others are picking on you, you'll also feel victimized. Since neither of these answers will eliminate the problem, it will keep recurring and you'll go on experiencing the same negative, self-defeating emotions you're feeling now.

Because we tend to see ourselves as we think others do, losing people's respect and friendship often leads to loss of self-respect and self-liking. While we may not hate those whom we disrespect or dislike, we generally don't care to associate with them. The situation is especially awkward when it is yourself whom you wish you could avoid.

***For better alternatives*** see the information about Answers 2 and 6.



*If you chose*

**1** go with the team but ask some of your teammates to tell you if you get out of line, or

**5** ask the bartender to stop serving you if you start to get loud

***You perceive the problem to be*** that no one stops you from having too much to drink.

*You think this because you believe* it is easier to handle problems with others' help.

*You believe it can best be solved by* getting someone to tell you when to quit drinking.

*PROBABLE OUTCOME:* You will continue to socialize with the team members after games, and when the guardians you've appointed tell you to quit drinking, you'll do one of the following:

> a) become belligerent or angry because they're trying to tell you what to do
>
> b) ignore the help you asked them to give you, or
>
> c) cooperate and limit your drinking as long as they are watching over you.

Instead of making things better for you, the others' assistance is only likely to make you resentful of their "interference."

*How is this likely to make you feel?* Resentful, angry, and blaming. By persuading others to be your nurse, baby-sitter, or keeper, you set them up to be either the bad guy when you want to keep drinking or the fall guy when you feel like ignoring their help. Despite requesting others' assistance, you'll resent them if they give it, blame them if they do not, and in general, feel as though the world has conspired against you.

*Will you feel good about yourself?* No. By relying on others to be your caretakers, you emphasize your weakness, dependency, and lack of self-control, which will lower your opinion of yourself.

*For better alternatives* see the information about Answers 2 and 6.

**LEVEL 3 ANSWERS**

*If you chose*

**2** tell Tom you've made other plans and then go home, or

**6** go along with the team and drink only soft drinks

*You perceive the problem to be* that you have allowed alcoholic beverages to have a negative effect on your life.

*You think this because you believe* you are responsible for your own behavior.

*You believe it can best be solved by* avoiding alcohol, at least when you're with the team.

*PROBABLE OUTCOME:* Since you will eliminate any offensive behavior on your part by going somewhere else or by drinking non-alcoholic beverages, you won't create a disturbance, the team will continue to be welcome at the pizza parlor, and you will continue to be welcome on the team.

*How is this likely to make you feel?* A little disappointed but, in general, happy, and relieved. Since you've derived a certain amount of pleasure from drinking with your friends, you'll miss doing it, but you can still enjoy the lively after-game conversations if you choose. And being the baseball enthusiast that you are, you will also be pleased because you'll be able to continue playing ball with other good athletes.

*Will you feel good about yourself?* Yes. By accepting responsibility for this problem instead of blaming others or asking for their help, you assume greater control over your life, increase your self-confidence, and move toward a more satisfying future. Realizing that you can successfully handle this problem on your own increases your good feelings about yourself.

# What's The *Real* Problem?

The problem is not that people are being unfair or unreasonable, it is Joe's unwillingness to acknowledge that *a)* he has a problem, and *b) he* created it. In short, he is reluctant to assume responsibility for his objectionable after-game behavior.

The Joe of Level 1 has convinced himself that he is blameless and that the problem originates in the narrow viewpoints of the restaurant managers and/or his teammates. This is a convenient position for him to assume, of course, because putting the blame on others eliminates any need for him to change, except for finding a more "compatible" group of people or limiting his contact with others.

The Level 2 Joe is aware that he is causing a problem, but in typical Level 2 fashion, he feels the responsibility for it should be spread around, so he tries to enlist the aid of the bartender or some of his teammates to solve it. There is an advantage to this approach because if he can convince others to assume responsibility for his actions, he will have handy scapegoats to blame when his drinking gets out of hand. The disadvantage to schemes of this sort is that they're usually not successful. Even if one of these answers *did* work, neither will eliminate the problem because the solution depends on others' help.

As the Level 3 Joe finally realized, part of maturing is understanding that at times he must face some hard personal truths. In this case, it is that he sometimes causes problems when he has been drinking alcohol. By accepting this fact and deciding to act on it, he acknowledged that *he* was responsible for his behavior. If he wanted to continue enjoying baseball with this team, he knew he had to change because he could not expect different results if he continued behaving as he had. Once he has discovered the cause of his problem and has taken appropriate steps to correct it, both he and his teammates will be much happier.

# Accepting Personal Responsibility

Responsibility, *n.* a detachable burden easily shifted to the shoulders of God, Fate, Fortune, Luck, or one's neighbor.
AMBROSE BIERCE, *The Devil's Dictionary*

To say we are less than excited at the idea of accepting personal responsibility is a great understatement because, for many of us, the term has too many unpleasant connotations. We hear people say things like, "You'll have to grow up and accept responsibility," or, "You're shirking your responsibility," or, "Haven't you any sense of responsibility?"

Because of comments like these, we decide taking responsibility must be distasteful, restricting and boring, a pleasureless activity to be avoided at all costs. We think, "It would probably involve me in all kinds of tedious duties and unpleasant matters. I'd better avoid it as long as I can."

This attitude is understandable because in many ways we've been discouraged from assuming personal responsibility. If we think about the role government, religion, and law enforcement play in our day-to-day existence, it becomes obvious they have assumed responsibility for some of the most important and meaningful areas of our lives. Instead of encouraging independence and self-direction, these entities have urged us to accept and conform. Besides these authoritarian influences, our social, educational, and organizational machinery operate in such a manner that many of us, even as adults, are accustomed to receiving the same kind of supervision we received as children. Keeping these facts in mind, it is not only reasonable that we should try to shirk responsibility, it is almost inevitable.

What happens when we try to turn our back on responsibility? We are besieged by problems, and many of them! In fact, almost all the difficulties we deal with on a daily basis were caused, in one way or another, by our failure to accept responsibility.

Think about the core problems in the scenarios: each originated in the central character's failure to accept a legitimate responsibility. Their problems wouldn't have occurred if

- Stan had realized it was *his* responsibility to look out for his best interests (Chapter 2)
- Carla had taken responsibility for fulfilling her own needs first (Chapter 3)
- Karen had taken responsibility for providing herself with approval (Chapter 4)
- Brian and Sally had taken responsibility for the financial obligation they incurred (Chapter 5)
- Richard had understood he was responsible for *his own* happiness, not his father's (Chapter 6)
- Mikki had assumed responsibility for providing herself with approval (Chapter 7)
- Melissa had realized it was her responsibility to accept Donna's differences, rather than change her (Chapter 8)
- Shana had taken responsibility for the safekeeping of her purse (Chapter 9)
- Connie had assumed the responsibility for providing herself with approval (Chapter 10)
- Joe had assumed responsibility for his behavior (Chapter 11)

The point these situations illustrate so clearly is this: it is usually to our advantage to accept personal responsibility rather than deny it.

## WHAT ARE OUR RESPONSIBILITIES?

This brings up an interesting question: just what *are* we responsible for? The answer is, for much more than we have generally assumed.

- *We are responsible for verifying the accuracy and validity of the values by which we live.* Directly or indirectly, most of us learned our rules for living from those around whom we grew up. Unfortunately, we uncritically absorbed unrealistic and possibly even destructive and inhumane ideas along with ideas of genuine benefit. This being true, it is in our best interests to give serious thought to the principles and precepts by which we live and then eliminate or replace those not derived from *our own* mature understanding of the issues involved. Because the rules we live by continually influence us, it is imperative we think them through carefully.

  *If we accept this responsibility,* we will be considered just, fair, and reasonable. Because we act on facts combined with compassionate understanding, we can go to sleep each night knowing we've behaved rationally and realistically and have dealt honestly and ethically with others and with ourselves.

  *If we refuse this responsibility,* we risk living by impractical, unrealistic, and potentially harmful ideas. Because our actions are not based on fact, we often make poor, ill-advised decisions that generate unnecessary sorrow and hardship for everyone involved.

- *We are responsible for providing our own approval.* It is easy to feel good about ourselves when others appear to like us, but to maintain our emotional equilibrium we must be able to feel just as good about ourselves when they don't. To acquire this highly desirable ability, we need to grasp both intellectually and emotionally that the only approval we genuinely *need* can and must be supplied from our inner resources.

*If we accept this responsibility,* we will experience a high level of happiness and contentment and enjoy life as we work to achieve our chosen goals, objectives, and pleasures. While we sympathize with those who believe they must ceaselessly earn others' good opinions, we maintain our self-respect, dignity, and peace of mind.

*If we refuse this responsibility,* we sacrifice our integrity on the altar of good opinion, giving up time, money, convenience, and power to bow, scrape, and fall all over ourselves trying to make people like us. Because we feel that pleasing others is essential, we tolerate their whims and moods, jump through the hoops they hold up for us, and in general, act as though we are not entitled to happiness and a life of our own.

- *We are responsible for understanding our motivation.* Why do we do what we do? Many of us are reluctant to investigate our motives because we're afraid of what we might find. If we are courageous enough to look, we will find generous, loving, and admirable ideas existing side-by-side with ideas we are ashamed to acknowledge or admit — even to ourselves. But it is precisely *because* we have these less-than-noble purposes that it is to our advantage to uncover them. Believing it is not our job to understand why we act as we do is perhaps the ultimate irresponsibility.

  *If we accept this responsibility,* we increase the clarity of our thought and behave more wisely and appropriately. Although a conscious examination of our motives may initially be somewhat disturbing and unflattering, it is best to acknowledge and accept our less-than-noble reasons since this will begin the process of eliminating them. Unhampered by the need to defend our actions or compensate others for the unpleasant effects of our unthinking behavior, we are free to pursue our personal agenda with greater enjoyment and fewer distractions.

*If we refuse this responsibility,* we behave unthinkingly and leave a wide swath of destruction, anger, and despair in our wake. Unaware of the urges that prompt us, we often work against ourselves and benefit no one. Lacking a clear sense of direction, we totter from one disaster to the next, with barely enough time between them for a deep breath. To the extent that we act without understanding *why,* we are a rudderless ship on a collision course with life.

- *We are responsible for creating our own happiness.* Contrary to what many of us believe, happiness doesn't just happen to us or occur because of someone or something outside us; it is a state of mind we establish through our attitude. Being happy is the result of a conscious or unconscious decision we have made about how we're going to view the world. While certain objects, circumstances, or people may seem to *cause* our happiness, in fact they can only *contribute* to it.

*If we accept this responsibility,* we create joy in our life. Understanding that *we* are the source of our happiness, we frame ourselves and our experiences positively, we center our thoughts on pleasant subjects, we interpret events in our favor, and we avoid unnecessary thinking about disturbing topics. If we become unhappy, we discover why and take whatever safe, legal, and ethical steps are necessary to change matters.

*If we refuse this responsibility,* happiness will be an occasional feeling instead of our customary state. Because we do not create happiness inside ourselves, we try to obtain it externally, believing it will be ours once we have acquired more possessions, greater honors, higher titles, or have met the right person. Since none of these attainments can actually provide the happiness we seek, we wither in a colorless, joyless world of disappointment and despair.

- *We are responsible for the emotions we experience.* Some of us think our emotional responses are beyond our control. We insist they're natural or instinctive or that they're inevitable reactions to others' actions or external events, but in most cases, this isn't true. Emotions originate *inside* us, not outside, and, with few exceptions are the result of choices we've made in the past about how we should feel under certain circumstances. Consequently, when we become angry, it's not because we must but because at one time or another we decided that at times it was appropriate or right to be angry. When we are sad, it's not because we have no other options, but because of the many alternatives available to us, we've chosen to feel unhappy.

  *If we accept responsibility for our emotions*, we avoid many counter-productive negative feelings and have an agreeable, less troubling emotional life. Knowing first impulses are often unwise, we try to avoid giving in to them. We observe and evaluate emotional reactions that cause us pain and practice (not always successfully) reacting from considered thought instead of habit. We understand that we gain greater control of our life by exerting some control over our emotions.

  *If we refuse this responsibility,* we may be elated one day, suicidal the next, and highly susceptible to moodiness, dejection and disappointment. We often feel picked on and blame others or life or God for treating us unfairly. By denying that *we* are in control, we allow ourselves to *be* controlled — by the weather, others' actions, or our childhood programming.

- *We are responsible for achieving our goals and desires.* The secret is out: there is no white knight, fairy godmother, or benign deity standing in the wings waiting for the perfect moment to enter our lives, solve our problems, provide us with our heart's desire, and ensure that we live happily ever after. While it is inevitable that we will sometimes need others' assistance to accomplish our objectives, it is primarily *our* efforts, *our* energy, and *our* determination that transform our dreams into reality.

*If we accept this responsibility,* we make our goals become reality through careful thinking, planning, and effort. Because we take responsibility for the direction our life takes and leave very little to chance, we usually achieve our goals. If opportunities don't present themselves, we create them! When things don't work out as we wish, we consider our options, intensify our efforts, and search for new solutions. To reach our goals, we take responsibility for where we are, who we are, and what we are. Because we are often successful, people say we are lucky. *We* know that the harder we work, the luckier we get.

*If we refuse this responsibility,* we are disappointed and unhappy much of the time. We complain a lot because *a)* we feel unfairly deprived of the things we most want and believe we deserve, and *b)* we're certain our inability to attain our desires is due to others' lack of enthusiasm, and we hope our complaining will goad them into action. Then, after we've spent our life vainly waiting for someone or something to come along and make everything wonderful for us, and when we are too old to do anything about it, we finally realize *the job was up to us all the time.* Too late we discover that merely wanting something does not bring us any closer to getting it.

- *We are responsible for learning from our mistakes and problems.* All of us make mistakes, but we don't all react to them in the same way. Some of us try to avoid blame by insisting our errors are due to others' actions or to adverse circumstances. Others of us more wisely turn mistakes to our advantage by thinking of them as opportunities to learn.

  *If we accept this responsibility,* we investigate the areas in which we have problems to discover the true cause of our mistakes.

Knowing we make errors only because we lack the understanding necessary to avoid them, we concentrate on acquiring or developing that understanding. We do this on a continuing basis, by analyzing our unpleasant experiences to determine where different actions on our part would have kept them from happening. By taking responsibility for mistakes or problems, we make them something we can fix.

*If we refuse this responsibility,* we are miserable creatures, indeed. Tormented by a seemingly endless series of problems, we try to engage others' sympathy as we make the same mistakes again and again. Because we fail to acknowledge that we played a part in creating our problems, we do not develop the new ideas and behavior necessary to avoid them in the future. When we deny responsibility for our mistakes, we forfeit the opportunity to learn from them and give up our power to change and improve matters.

- *We are responsible for our health and physical well-being.* While it is tempting to leave all matters of physical health entirely in the hands of medical professionals, it is unwise for several reasons. *First,* most doctors are trained to cure us of illnesses *after* we get them, rather than help us avoid them in the first place. *Second,* new treatments, medications, and research are increasing far faster than most physicians can keep up with them.

*If we accept this responsibility,* we stay informed on health matters because we realize that no one has as much at stake as we do. We learn about exercise, nutrition, lifestyle, and their impor-tance to our overall well-being and then put the information to work for us. We don't begrudge the time this takes because we consider it an investment that will repay itself again and again. - Although there will be times when problems make it necessary to seek professional help, intelligent and knowledgeable behavior on our part can make those instances rare.

*If we refuse this responsibility,* we set the stage for frequent, possibly fatal illnesses. Without attention to the fuel we provide our bodies, we may lack essential nutrients and ingest products which can cause physical damage. Lacking proper exercise, our bones will weaken, our range of motion grow smaller, and our weight increase. If we abuse our body, the mistreated parts will wear out prematurely. We can look forward to a future that includes the possibility of great pain, immobility, dependency, and possible financial ruin.

- *We are responsible for paying our own way.* No matter what kind of skills we have or how well we've developed them, unless we have an incapacitating illness or handicap, we are obligated to use them to provide our livelihood. Others work to serve *their* purposes, not ours, and they rightly feel they have no obligation to give us things we are capable of getting for ourselves. As adults, we must understand that furnishing our financial support is no one's job but our own.

*If we accept this responsibility,* we live on money we've earned ourselves or that is legitimately ours. And whether we've chosen a Spartan existence or an extremely luxurious one, we live within the financial limits *we've* set, not those dictated by others. If we're unhappy with the amount of income we currently receive, instead of looking for a handout, we'll devise honest ways to increase it.

*If we refuse this responsibility,* we play "poor little me" throughout life, trying to convince others to support us. We regard people's benevolence not as something we are obligated to repay, but as a donation given us because we're too inept to take care of ourselves.

Because we've abdicated control of our income, others decide how much money we should receive and when we should receive it. We do not live as we choose, but as we are allowed to. Although we may congratulate ourselves on getting others to pay our share, our cleverness robs us of dignity and self-respect. When we look in the mirror, we see a second-class citizen peering back at us.

- *We are responsible for the quality of our relationships.* Good relationships rarely occur by accident. Usually, they exist because we have chosen to give up a certain amount of individuality and independence in exchange for benefits we anticipate receiving from our association with others.

*If we accept this responsibility,* our relationships are open and honest and based on mutual respect. We give as willingly as we receive. We consider other human beings as important and worthwhile as ourselves, and we respect and tolerate their differences. Because we don't expect people to take care of us or take the blame for us, we appreciate them for what they are and not for how we can use them. We don't waste time or cause problems trying to change others because we understand that people will change only when they perceive it is to their advantage.

We also understand that, with the exception of those related to us by blood, we are not in relationships because we're compelled to be but because we have *chosen* to be. And because we understand we are responsible for the quality of our relationships, we terminate those we find to be harmful or destructive.

*If we refuse this responsibility,* our relationships with others are likely to be exploitive and unsatisfying. We remain in damaging relationships because we're receiving a payoff of some sort (even if we are not consciously aware of it) or because we have not yet realized we *can* free ourselves from them.

We commonly believe that *1)* when relationships become bitter, it is not our fault, and *2)* people have an obligation to become more like we want them to be. Our circle of friends consists primarily of those we can take advantage of and those who can take advantage of us. Because we believe the success of our relationships is not our responsibility, we lose friends, partners, and mates and endure strained friendships and broken, bitter marriages.

- ***We are responsible for our self-esteem.*** We cannot rely on external sources to provide us with the self-respect, self-approval, self-liking, and self-confidence we need. To be effective, the recognition that we are decent, worthwhile, and deserving human beings must come from inside us, not from others' comments.

  *If we accept this responsibility,* we reject self-defeating behavior in favor of actions which reinforce or increase our good feelings about ourselves. We choose the company of those whom we enjoy as they are, feeling no need to seek out friends who will make us feel good about ourselves. We provide our own emotional support instead of seeking it from others. Rather than doing what others think we should, we do what *we* think is best. By assuming control of our self-esteem, we affirm and reinforce our belief in our own worth.

  *If we refuse this responsibility,* we depend on external sources to provide us with good feelings about ourselves. We try to buy others' compliments and admiration with accomplishments or education, or by enhancing our appearance. We choose our goals, not because we value them ourselves but because we believe *others* do. Because we rely on others for emotional support, we are emotionally vulnerable and often feel disappointed, unappreciated, and unworthy.

- *We are responsible for accepting reality.* We are not obligated to like reality, but we must acknowledge its existence and deal with it as well as we can. When confronted with facts, there is no reasonable course of action open to us but to accept that which is unalterably true because to not do so is dangerous and delusional.

  *If we accept this responsibility,* we are firmly grounded in WHAT IS. Instead of indulging in hopes and fantasies, we deal in facts and probabilities. We are rarely disappointed, not because we never fail but because we avoid unrealistic expectations. We work with what has happened, not what we *wish* had happened. We understand that the more we distort reality, the more confused and unmanageable our life grows.

  *If we refuse this responsibility,* we waste a great deal of time thinking about the way things were and the way they ought to be. Because we turn a blind eye to facts and neglect to take action to bring our fancies to fruition, we have little to show for our dreaming but disappointment. Limited in many ways by self-delusion, we rely on those who are more reality-oriented to remedy our deficiencies and make up for our shortcomings.

What is the inevitable result of failing to accept these responsibilities? It is this:

> **We lose control of every aspect of our life**
> **for which we disclaim responsibility.**

In short, whatever we do not control, controls us.

## WHERE DOES IT ALL END?

If the idea of assuming personal responsibility is a new one, it may seem like a pretty overwhelming project and one we probably feel ill-prepared to start. And it would be false to say that acquiring a sense of personal responsibility is a painless and trouble-free process because it is not. It would be *true,* however, to say that living *without* a sense of personal responsibility is far worse than any problems we may encounter acquiring one.

Fortunately, taking responsibility is not an all-or-nothing proposition. We do not have to immediately become accountable for everything. We can do what we've always done when learning new skills: begin modestly and work our way up.

As our sense of responsibility increases, we'll find that *the more responsibility we accept, the easier accepting it becomes.* Before long, we'll realize that not only is being self-responsible not boring or restricting, it is actually quite pleasant and we are far happier than we've ever been. Why? Strangely, once we begin widening the scope of our responsibility, we discover that many obligations we once thought were ours, are not! Paradoxically, taking responsibility for our life actually liberates us, and the more personal responsibility we accept, the more free we become.

As a whole, we humans have one primary goal: to be happy. And although this desire exists in all of us, human diversity makes us attempt to satisfy it in millions of different ways. But no matter which bright butterfly we chase, it will bring us happiness *only* if we feel in control of our life. Because this idea is so important, if you do not remember any other words from this chapter, memorize these:

**I control only those aspects of my life<br>
for which I accept responsibility.**

## *Important Ideas to Consider*

- Since my happiness is closely related to how much responsibility I accept, the more responsibility I take the happier I become.

- Ultimately, every aspect of my life is my own responsibility.

- I will stop feeling submissive and dependent when I understand that I am accountable for my life.

- If I do not assume responsibility for my life, no one, with the possible exception of the government, will.

- Assuming personal responsibility gives me real power and increases my competence, effectiveness, and inner strength.

- The more accountability I refuse, the more chaotic my life becomes.

- I am *where* I am and the *way* that I am because of my past decisions.

- If I wish to promote positive change in my life, I must change the way I make my decisions.

- There are many other choices and options available to me if I choose to take them.

- Other people create their own emotions, just as I do.

## *Questions to Ask Yourself*

- Do I spend more time blaming others for my problems than I do in trying to solve them?

- How often do I feel and act like a victim?

- Do I rely on others' opinions?

- Do I object to taking responsibility for where and what I am? If I do, whose responsibility do I think it is?

- Do I feel as though my life is outside my control and I am just an innocent victim of circumstances?.

- Do I accept responsibility for my errors in judgment?

- When things go wrong do I ask myself what I could have done to have made them better?

# CHAPTER 12

# A Short Course in Solving Problems

## WHY WE HAVE PROBLEMS

The problems outlined in this book's scenarios, like most of our problems, arise because one or more of the following conditions are true:

1) we act on incorrect beliefs or unrealistic expectations

2) we place too much importance on others' approval

3) we undervalue ourselves and our worth as a person

4) we neglect responsibilities that are rightfully ours.

Obviously, then, to avoid creating problems, we need to

1) expose our incorrect beliefs and unrealistic expectations as the inaccuracies they are

2) learn to provide our own approval, so we do not feel others' approval is essential

3) gain a truer assessment of our value as a human being

4) accept the responsibilities that are legitimately ours.

How can we accomplish these objectives?

## DEVELOPING ALTERNATIVE SOLUTIONS

There are three different methods we can use to improve our problem-solving/preventing skills and eliminate many problems from our lives. We can

1) improve our self-esteem

2) "remodel" our personality, or

3) learn to live by "the rules."

Although each of these paths leads to the same place, they begin quite differently.

# METHOD 1
## *Improving your self-esteem*

There are three incorrect core beliefs at the heart of poor self-esteem.

> 1) I am a victim
>
> 2) I am inadequate
>
> 3) I am essentially bad.

When you repudiate these inaccurate beliefs and the sub-beliefs that reinforce them and replace them with beliefs in keeping with reality, you'll find many of your problems disappear almost magically. This happens because, with an improved opinion of yourself, you are less concerned about others' opinions and have greater confidence in yourself and your problem-solving skills.

Some people believe it is possible to improve your feelings about yourself by stressing your uniqueness as an individual and stuffing your head full of essentially meaningless phrases about how wonderful you are. This is largely ineffective because it tries to make you feel good without first getting rid of the reasons you feel bad. All you're likely to get from this approach is an emotional hangover.

Keep in mind that you cannot pour anything into a full cup. If you wish to improve your feelings about yourself, you must remove the mental reasons why you feel bad about yourself, and then your self-esteem will automatically increase.

If you choose this method, check the "Suggested Reading" section at the end of this book, and visit your local library or bookstore for books on the subject. Keep your eyes and ears open for information about seminars or workshops in your area. A small investment of time spent improving your self-esteem will produce major dividends in your life.

# Method 2
## *Remodeling your personality*

If this idea sounds pretty overwhelming, take heart: it doesn't all have to be done in one day, or for that matter, it doesn't all have to be done. Using this approach, you make gradual changes in yourself and in how you see the world and other people. As you gain greater understanding and widen your perspective, you'll become aware of answers you would never have considered before.

You can begin this process by doing the exercises found at the end of most chapters. Start with the first scenario or pick one that has special significance for you. Work with each exercise for one week, and at the end of that week, assess its effect on you and your attitude.

Here are some other helpful activities and attitudes:

•*Enlarge your library of responses.* Since the way you respond to problems depends on how well you understand them, the wider your understanding of a situation, the more likely you are to select a workable solution. To add to your possible responses, do this: think of five people you know, including at least one person you do not like. Imagine each of these people in problem situations like those in which you often find yourself. How would each of them solve your problems? In what ways would their responses differ from yours? Whose response is most likely to produce the most satisfying results? The more aware you become of alternative responses, the more likely you are to find answers that will work.

•*Stop thinking about yourself so much.* Don't waste time wondering what other people think of you; they're usually too busy thinking about themselves and their problems to spare you even a few moments. Don't waste time moaning about how awful life is because it makes problems seem even worse. Get involved in activities that give you less time to think about yourself and your problems. Become a volunteer, take up a hobby, join a club, or do all three. Don't waste time on self-pity, no matter how bad things seem; telling yourself how powerless you are only weakens you further.

• *Begin setting realistic goals for yourself.* If you don't know what you want, you're not likely to get it. In other words, you are most likely to obtain what you want if you set specific goals. If the idea of goal-setting is new to you, begin with tiny ones, just to get the practice of setting and achieving goals. Once you gain control of your life in small ways, you can make your goals increasingly more ambitious. If you act without specific goals, it's anyone's guess as to what you might accomplish.

• *Take the initiative.* If you're not getting what you want out of life, instead of sitting passively by waiting for good things to happen to you, *make* them happen. Just as with goals, take small steps to begin with, and once acting on your own no longer feels so strange and uncomfortable, move up to bigger and bigger challenges. Become an actor on the stage of life, instead of remaining in the audience.

• *Refuse to think of yourself as a victim.* Why picture yourself at your weakest when you can think of yourself much more powerfully? Instead of feeling defeated when something unpleasant happens to you, explore the situation from different angles to see how you can extract some benefit from what occurred. Discovering a benefit, however small, lifts you out of the victim category.

• *Choose to be happy.* Since you can choose which emotions to feel, how you experience your life is pretty much up to you. If you are miserable, it is because you have chosen to be, not because you must.

If you radiate joy, it is because you understand you're a cause, not an effect. It is not what actually happens to you but how you perceive it that determines how you feel. You are free to change your perception at any time.

• *Make peace with reality.* Since the world isn't run to please us, we must sometimes deal with pain, difficulty, and loss. When you are involved in situations you truly have no power to change, you need to remember that life is impartial. It doesn't play favorites, although those who learn from their errors may make it seem so. The more you insist on classifying some events in your life as bad or unacceptable, the more you make yourself miserable.

• *Determine to solve most of your problems yourself.* When faced with a problem, it is simplest to immediately assume that *you* are the person best qualified to solve it. Like everyone else, you possess reserves of inner strength that can help you meet life on its own terms. Unless you are prepared to offer others an incentive they value in exchange for their help, it's best not to count on their assistance.

• *Realize you always have choices.* When it comes to solving problems, perhaps our greatest need is to realize that *we are not limited to doing things the way we've always done them.* You can change your responses any time you decide to by choosing more effective behavior, more realistic ways of reacting, and more productive states of mind. When old patterns of behavior do not produce positive results, it's time to develop new ones.

• *Examine your thoughts and feelings.* Rather than reacting mechanically when problems arise, search your mind for the ideas and emotions that cause you to create them. When you become aware of the thoughts that prompt your unwise behavior, you will find they generally stem from old habits of thought that you acquired when you were too young or inexperienced to evaluate their appropriateness.

• *Don't blame others for your problems.* Instead of dwelling on people's meanness and complaining about the awful things they do to you, think about how you may have contributed to or created your problems yourself. As long as you insist others cause your problems, you will never solve them. Successful problem resolution is not a matter of rearranging things and people around you but internalizing the problem and solution and making it one you can solve.

•*Don't consider avoidance a solution.* Staying out of the way of certain people may seem like the best way to prevent some problems, and sometimes it is. Usually, though, it merely postpones your finding the real solution, which means you're likely to experience the same problem in the future with other people. Another disadvantage of avoidance is that it's sometimes impossible or impractical to avoid people such as family members or co-workers with whom you are in daily contact.

• *Learn from your mistakes.* You can't expect to solve future problems without a certain amount of reflection on those in your past. Most of the troublesome situations you've experienced have this in common: at some point, as they were developing you could have avoided the problem entirely by doing or saying something other than what you did. Whenever a problem occurs, ask yourself, "At what point would a different action on my part have prevented this situation from occurring?"

• *Become aware of consequences.* When you're thinking of how to solve a problem, ask yourself *first,* what kind of risks are involved in your solution, and *second,* what the short-term and long-term effects of your choices are likely to be. Realizing that certain actions almost inevitably produce undesirable results can serve as a powerful deterrent.

214

If you give no thought to what might occur as a result of your solution, you may make matters worse than they were to begin with.

• *Look for patterns in your problems.* Carefully think through the problems that keep recurring in your life. Although details may make each one seem unique, the attitudes, ideas, and behavior that prompt them tend to be the same. If you take the time to think about exactly what happened when things went badly for you, you can often uncover a pattern, enabling you to avoid similar problems in the future.

If you make each of these ideas a project for a few weeks, you'll soon notice positive changes and improvements in your life.

# Method 3
## *Learning "The Rules"*

Just as the ineffective answers from Levels 1 and 2 have certain characteristics in common, so do the effective answers from Level 3. We can refer to these characteristics as guidelines, standards, or rules, but whatever we call them, once we know and understand these principles, we can apply them to current problems to forecast how well our answers will work.

Prior to using a particular response, you can determine that it will be effective if it meets these six criteria:

Rule 1: *Your solution must make you feel good, or at least not bad about yourself and the situation*

Rule 2: *Your solution may not be intended to injure, harm, or put anyone at risk physically or emotionally*

Rule 3: *Your solution must eliminate the problem entirely or allow you to reclassify it as a "non-problem"*

Rule 4: *Your solution may not require anyone other than yourself to change or behave differently*

Rule 5: *Your solution must give your personal welfare and convenience priority over others'*

Rule 6: *Your solution may not require anyone to assume a responsibility that is legitimately yours.*

Do these rules seem restricting? They're intended to be. They limit you to only solutions that will work. If you deviate from them in favor of a Level 1 or Level 2 answer, you will not solve your problem. On the other hand, if you follow them

- you'll stop experiencing the same problems again and again
- you'll eliminate much frustration from your life

- your relationships will be happier, more satisfying, and more rewarding
- you will dispose of mental refuse that has troubled you for years
- you will solve personal problems more rapidly and effectively than ever before.

## HOW THESE RULES WORK

To find out how these principles can help you solve your problems, read through the sample problems below. By applying the six Rules to each answer, you can weigh advantages and disadvantages. Here are some problems to illustrate how these Rules work.

**Sample problem:** You are dining with a new acquaintance in a popular restaurant. Although the food is excellent and your dinner companion's conversation is stimulating, his noisy eating and poor table manners bother you greatly. What is the smartest thing to do?

LEVEL 1 ANSWER: *Vow to never eat with this person again?* This answer fails to meet Rule 1 (you won't feel any better about yourself or the situation) and 3 (even if you never see this particular individual again, you are bound to encounter others like him.)

LEVEL 2 ANSWER: *Politely tell your acquaintance it's extremely rude to make noises while eating?* This solution fails to meet rule 2 (you are attempting to make the other person uncomfortable enough to change his behavior), and 3 (it will not eliminate the problem), and 4 (you are expecting someone other than you to change).

LEVEL 3 ANSWER: *Realize that you must change your attitude about others' table manners if you want to avoid causing yourself discomfort?* This is the only solution that meets all Rules.

**Sample problem:** You've gone to the mall to do some shopping. As you near the shop you're looking for, you see someone who you know dislikes you approaching from the opposite direction. You immediately become uncomfortable because when you've encountered her before, she has made a point of being extremely unpleasant, even when there were other people around. This time is no exception. Even though there are a number of other shoppers near when you pass each other, she loudly calls you rude, highly unflattering names. Would it be best to:

LEVEL 1 ANSWER: *Call her names in return?* This answer doesn't satisfy Rule 1 (if you feel good, it will be only briefly), 2 (you are attempting to make the other person feel bad in order to get her to change her behavior), and 3 (it will not eliminate or diminish the problem, but it will make you look as ill-mannered as the other person and almost certainly guarantee a return shouting match when next you meet.)

LEVEL 2 ANSWER: *Stop and reason with her, and try to get her to stop calling you names?* This answer doesn't satisfy conditions 3 (it's not entirely impossible that talking with her might alleviate *this* problem, but it won't prevent the same kind of problem from happening with others) or 4 (it requires someone other than yourself to change behavior).

LEVEL 3 ANSWER: *Smile, say "Hello," and keep on walking?* This answer will work because it satisfies all conditions. Rather than thinking badly of you, anyone witnessing the incident would probably decide, not that you deserve the names the woman called you, but that she is a badly disturbed individual.

If you are accustomed to using mostly Level 1 and Level 2 answers, the Level 3 solutions will probably seem unusual and far-fetched at first. "I couldn't do this," you think. "This is too hard." "This kind of answer would be totally out of character for me." "This is asking too much of me," or some other obstructive thought.

Because much of our behavior is prompted by negative emotions, we may feel that giving up the emotional responses of Levels 1 and 2 will remove something important from our life. We may even feel we're giving up something of value in exchange for some abstract, theoretical uncertainty. While it is true that we must eliminate certain kinds of behavior when we choose Level 3 solutions, it is a fairly painless process, and what we relinquish is only behavior that makes everyone miserable.

The Level 3 responses are not some weird, impractical, fantasy ideas dreamed up to entertain you, but the options happy people choose on a regular basis. We might even say, choosing Level 3 responses is largely the reason that happy people *are* happy. So the real question is, "Do you want to be happier?"

What's your answer?

# Appendix

## THE THREE LEVELS OF PROBLEM-SOLVING
## AND THOSE WHO CHOOSE THEM

If you think about the scenarios and answers in the first part of this book, you will realize that even though the solutions from the same level differ in particulars, each level has unique characteristics that distinguish it from the other two.

And just as all answers originating from the same level share certain characteristics, people who typically respond from the same level share certain beliefs, thought patterns, attitudes, and coping mechanisms. In actual practice, however, no one solves problems from only one level. We may center our problem-solving efforts in Level 2, for instance, but in daily life, we shift from one level to another many times a day, and sometimes in merely seconds.

Here is an examination of each of the three levels of problem-solving, listing first, the dominant features of its solutions, and second, personal characteristics of those who most often choose solutions from that level.

## *Level 1 Responses to Problems:*

**Distinguishing characteristic:** *Addressing the wrong problem.* Level 1 approaches address peripheral issues rather than actual problems. Sometimes we sense these responses aren't particularly good ones, but we use them anyway because we can't think of any better alternatives.

**Why we choose responses from Level 1:** We are immersed in our problems much of the time, so we see things from a self-centered viewpoint that keeps us from becoming aware of and considering more helpful options. Because our problem-solving efforts often fail, we sometimes try highly unlikely answers, feeling that it doesn't make any difference what we try because nothing will work anyway.

**Likelihood of success:** *Poor.* Trying to resolve difficulties using this kind of approach is like painting your house to make your roof stop leaking. Because Level 1 responses usually focus on unimportant or non-existent predicaments instead of actual problems, results are generally unsatisfactory.

**Disadvantages of using:** If Level 1 answers *do* produce positive results (which is unlikely), it is generally by accident. If we habitually use Level 1 responses, we probably feel we've been singled out for a long run of bad luck when, in fact, our lack of success has been due to our failure to examine our problems from different viewpoints.

## *Personal Characteristics of People Using Level 1 Responses*

**Typical emotions:** Because of the poor results we achieve when we address problems from this level, we often experience anger, disappointment, frustration, depression and self-pity. We spend a great deal of time thinking about how bad things are and how unfairly the world treats us. Sometimes we try to make ourselves feel better by using drugs or alcohol, but generally, they cause us to feel even worse. On a happiness scale of 1 through 10, with 1 being quite unhappy and 10 being quite happy, we center around 3 or 4.

**Self-confidence:** Since Level 1 approaches commonly fail, we have little confidence in ourselves or our abilities and are inclined to give up easily.

**Resourcefulness:** Believing our problem-solving skills to be severely limited, we are excessively and unnecessarily dependent on others' help. Instead of looking for a solution, we usually seek someone's assistance or a good excuse. Since we consider ourselves less-than-adequate, our problems often remain unsolved unless someone solves them for us.

**Acceptance of personal responsibility:** When problems arise, our primary concern is avoiding blame. Refusing accountability, we deny making errors and ignore or play down our contribution to problems. When we are not berating God or Life for our predicaments, we tend to blame anyone even remotely connected to them.

**Sense of being in control:** We feel in charge only a small amount of the time and wrongly believe that what happens to us is largely unavoidable. Because we feel victimized when our Level 1 responses fail, we view life from a defeatist viewpoint and consider failure almost inevitable. Since we habitually feel helpless and inadequate, life is anxiety-filled and painfully uncertain.

**Use of mistakes as learning tools:** Because we are in the habit of blaming our problems on external causes we rarely learn from our errors and, as a consequence, experience the same kinds of problems again and again. By denying responsibility for our mistakes, we close our minds to ideas that could produce positive change.

**In our relationships with others, we**

- place a great deal of importance on their approval
- think they don't experience things with the same emotional depth or intensity that we do
- consider their needs and rights far less important than our own
- fear and dislike them if they are different

- create problems by being judgmental
- blame them for many of our problems

**In our daily life we**
- feel threatened by new ideas
- are closely tied to events in the past
- strongly resist change
- ignore facts we dislike
- expect to achieve our **goals by** hoping, wishing, and persuading rather than doing
- become extremely upset when unexpected events disrupt our plans
- have a predominantly negative view of things
- approach problems with familiar responses that have never worked in the past

**We usually**
- are self-absorbed
- think of ourselves as victims
- have a generally poor opinion of ourselves
- are afraid to deviate too much from what we consider "normal" behavior
- feel emotionally injured by failures
- remain a slave to harmful habits

**Typical remarks**

"I don't know how."

"It's not my fault."

"I didn't do it."

"I couldn't help it."

"I can't handle it."

"Nobody understands me."

"This is too hard."

"It isn't fair."

"I never get the breaks."

"I can't change."

"I just have bad luck."

"My life is one disappointment after another."

"If it weren't for him (or her) I'd...."

"Why do people keep causing problems for me?"

"Why do I put up with this?"

## *Level 2 Responses to Problems*

**Distinguishing characteristic:** *relying on others' help to solve our problems.* When we respond from this level, we try to convince others to either *a)* solve our problems for us, or *b)* at the very least, help *us* solve them. Obviously, then, these tactics work only if we can persuade others to do as we ask. (Do not confuse this with *cooperation,* in which we offer others something they want in exchange for their assistance.)

**Why we choose responses from Level 2:** Generally, we ask for assistance because

1. We believe another person is causing the problem and should have to solve it

2. We want someone else who can take the blame if our solution doesn't work

3. We don't feel we are capable of dealing with it ourselves.

**Likelihood of success:** *Small.* Although Level 2 answers sometimes succeed, making others a part of our solution usually means the problem will be alleviated only briefly, if at all. In general, we can characterize Level 2 approaches as ideas which might conceivably work, but are probably short-term solutions at best.

**Disadvantages of using Level 2 answers:** If a Level 2 response actually works, it's usually for a limited amount of time. Consequently, those who use it have to solve the same problem again and again, if not in the same setting, then in a new one.

## *Personal Characteristics of People Using Level 2 Responses*

**Typical emotions:** Because we try to involve others in Level 2 responses, we are often disappointed by what we consider to be people's unreliability and reluctance to do what is right. When others refuse to help us with our problems, we may respond to their unwillingness or indifference with anger, frustration, depression and self-pity. On a happiness scale of 1 through 10, we center between 4 and 7.

**Self-confidence:** Since those of us who regularly choose Level 2 answers solve at least some of our problems, we have a moderate amount of faith in our ourselves and our abilities. Because of the unpredictability of our responses, our own assessment of our abilities may fall anywhere on the spectrum between *inadequate* and *well-qualified*, depending on how successful we were in our last attempt to solve a problem.

**Resourcefulness:** We feel our problem-solving ability is limited only by others' reluctance to do what they should.

**Acceptance of personal responsibility:** We enjoy taking the credit for praiseworthy activities, but when things go badly, we try to place the blame elsewhere. Although we prefer to point the finger of blame at others, if pressed and it is unavoidable, we may reluctantly accept partial responsibility. Because we believe others to be the cause of many of our problems, we think they, and not we, should have to solve them.

**Sense of being in control:** Because of limited success in resolving our difficulties, we feel in control now and then.

**Use of mistakes as learning tools:** Since we learn from our mistakes only if we acknowledge making them (and we rarely do), we are remarkably resistant to life's lessons.

**In our relationships with others, we**
- believe we are objective enough to judge them accurately
- place unnecessary importance on their approval
- blame them for many of our problems
- think their needs and rights are less important than our own
- try to convince them to help us reach our goals
- consider it acceptable to manipulate them to achieve our ends
- tolerate only minor deviations from "normal" behavior

**In our daily life we**
- accept change when it seems inevitable
- accept reality only reluctantly when we dislike it
- are often uncomfortable with new ideas
- find it difficult to adjust to unexpected events
- try new solutions only when we must
- think life alternates between positive and negative episodes

**We usually**
- dislike being shown we are wrong
- place too much emphasis on the past
- spend too much time thinking about ourselves

- find it hard to break harmful habits
- believe we have more problems than most people
- feel good about ourselves part of the time
- prefer to demonstrate our individuality in socially acceptable ways

**Typical remarks:**

"There's a problem I'd like to discuss with you."

"I need a favor."

"It would mean so much to me if you'd..."

"It's not my fault, it's *yours*."

"It wasn't my idea."

"I didn't do it."

"She/He is the one who started it!"

"Why are you doing this to me?"

"I'm tired of the way you're behaving."

"Your actions leave something to be desired."

"You've got a problem"

"Because I said so."

**Distinguishing characteristic:** *Self-reliance.* Although we are sometimes tempted to blame our problems on external causes or other people, we generally (and wisely) feel that if we want the job done properly, we must do it ourselves.

**Why we choose responses from this level:** Through either patient observation or trial and error, we have discovered we are the best and possibly the *only* person who can effectively solve our problems. No one else has the insight into our personal problems that *we* have, so we feel it is safest to be our own authority.

**Likelihood of success:** *Excellent.* Because Level 3 solutions concentrate on what *we* can do, they almost always work, and we are rarely disappointed.

**Disadvantages of using Level 3 answers:** We may be considered too independent by people who choose mainly Level 1 or Level 2 answers. Since those who center in Level 3 are most comfortable associating with others who center in the same Level, this is not usually a major concern.

## *Personal Characteristics of People Using Level 3 Responses*

**Typical emotions:** Since solutions devised from this level usually eliminate problems permanently, those of us who use it ordinarily feel happy and satisfied, enjoying a life that is relatively stress-free and uncomplicated. On a happiness scale of 1 through 10, we center around 8 or 9.

**Self-confidence:** Because we're accustomed to handling our own problems, we have a healthy belief in our own abilities. We expect to succeed and usually do. We think of failure as a challenge and keep trying until we are satisfied.

**Resourcefulness:** We are willing to experiment and, rather than trying to keep things as they are, we often ask ourselves how we might do things differently, more quickly, better, more efficiently, more enjoyably, or less stressfully.

**Acceptance of personal responsibility:** As long as they are legitimately ours, we are not shy about accepting responsibility for either good decisions or bad. Because we consider ourselves accountable for much of what occurs to us, we understand that we, and not others, must deal with our problems.

**Sense of being in control:** Believing we are responsible for the direction our life takes, we feel a great sense of control.

**Use of mistakes as learning tools:** When we make errors, we do what we can to discover what we did wrong, and then use that knowledge to avoid similar situations in the future. Instead of thinking of them as failures, we regard mistakes as good opportunities to improve the quality of our life.

**In our relationships with others we**
- avoid trying to impose our values on them
- are unconcerned about their disapproval unless it's essential for survival
- consider their needs and rights as important as our own
- accept and appreciate differences
- believe their feelings and aspirations are just as important as ours

**In our daily life we**

- are flexible
- tolerate, welcome, or enjoy change
- have a comfortable acceptance of reality
- believe we control the course of our lives
- are interested in new ideas and alternatives
- keep our thoughts primarily in the present
- think that life is what we make it
- believe we create most of our own problems
- try fresh solutions when old ones fail
- take direct action to achieve our goals

**We usually**

- admit our mistakes without reluctance
- discontinue practices we discover are harmful
- think more about what we do than about ourselves
- have self-respect and self-liking
- have a strong sense of individuality

**Typical remarks made by people using this level:**

"Oh, *that's* how it works!"

"Can you show me what I've been doing wrong?"

"I know I can do better."

"I can do this myself."

"It's not really hard."

"I deserve something better and I'm going to get it."

"No, thanks, I don't want to."

"It is your right to think anything you wish."

"Thanks, but I can do it myself."

"It's up to me to do something about this."

"It's my fault, so I'll take care of it."

"It's something I have to do myself."

"I caused this problem myself."

"It's my responsibility."

# Recommended Reading


Arapakis, Maria, *Softpower: How to Speak Up, Set Limits, and Say No Without Losing Your Lover, Your Job, or Your Friends.* New York: Warner Books, 1990.

Berry, Carmen Renee, *When Helping You is Hurting Me.* New York: Harper & Row, Publishers, 1988.

Brinkman, Dr. Rick, and Dr. Rick Kirschener, *Dealing With People You Can't Stand: How to Bring Out the Best in People at Their Worst.* New York: McGraw-Hill, Inc., 1994.

Branden, Nathaniel, *Taking Responsibility: Self-Reliance and the Accountable Life.* New York: Simon & Schuster, 1996.

Dawson, Roger, *13 Secrets of Power Performance.* New York: Prentice Hall, 1994.

Fox, Robin Lane, *The Unauthorized Version: Truth and Fiction in the Bible.* New York: Alfred A. Knopf, 1991.

Funk, Robert Walter, *Honest to Jesus: Jesus For a New Millennium.* Sonoma, California: Polebridge Press, 1996.

Gawain, Shakti, *Creative Visualization.* New York: Bantam Books, 1978.

Glasser, William, M.D., *Take Effective Control of Your Life.* New York: Harper & Row, 1984.

Goulston, Mark, M.D., and Philip Goldberg, *Get Out of Your Own Way: Overcoming Self-Defeating Behavior.* New York: The Berkley Publishing Group, 1996.

Greenwald, Dr. Harold, and Elizabeth Rich, *The Happy Person: A Seven-Step Plan.* New York: Avon Books, 1984.

Harrill, Susan E., M.Ed., *You Could Feel Good.* Houston, TX: Innerworks Publishing, 1987.

Hyatt, Carole, and Linda Gottlieb, *When Smart People Fail*. New York: Simon & Schuster, Inc., 1987.

McMahon, Susanna, Ph. D., *The Portable Therapist*. New York: Dell Publishing, 1992.

McWilliams, Peter, *Ain't Nobody's Business If You Do: The Absurdity of Consensual Crimes in a Free Society*. Los Angeles, CA: Prelude Press, 1993.

Minchinton, Jerry, *Maximum Self-Esteem: The Handbook For Reclaiming Your Sense of Self-Worth*. Vanzant, MO: Arnford House, 1993.
—*52 Things You Can Do To Raise Your Self-Esteem*. Vanzant, MO: Arnford House, 1994.

Semigran, Candace, *One-Minute Self-Esteem: Caring For Yourself and Others*. New York: Bantam, 1988.

## Works Cited

Balsekar, Ramesh S., *Explorations Into the Eternal*. Durham, NC: The Acorn Press, 1987.

# About the Author

Perpetually curious, author Jerry Minchinton has read extensively about self-esteem, motivation, and Eastern philosophies and religions. He combines the insight he's gained from these studies with practical business experience to shed light on some age-old problems of human behavior.

Jerry earned a B.A. with Highest Honors and a M.A. in Music at Eastern Washington University. An accomplished musician, he performed professionally for a number of years before founding a mail processing company. After guiding the firm through twelve years of steady growth, he withdrew from his CEO position to devote more time to the study of self-esteem and related subjects.

He has also written *Maximum Self-Esteem: The Handbook For Reclaiming Your Sense of Self-Worth,* and *52 Things You Can Do To Raise Your Self-Esteem,* both published by Arnford House..

A native of Wisconsin and a long-time resident of the Pacific Northwest, Jerry now lives and works in the beautiful Ozark Mountains of Southern Missouri.

**Order Form**

TELEPHONE: Call 1 (417) 261-2559, or toll-free 1(888) 709-2559.
FAX: 1 (417) 261-2559.
E-MAIL: arnford@townsqr.com
MONEY ORDERS: Mail to  Arnford House, Publishers
Route 1, Box 27
Vanzant, MO 65768

Please send me

_______ copies of  *Maximum Self-Esteem*          @ $14.95 ea.    _______________

_______ copies of  *52 Things You Can Do to*       @ $ 6.50 ea.    _______________
*Raise Your Self-Esteem*

_______ copies of  *Wising Up*                      @ $14.50 ea.    _______________

Shipping*    _______________

TOTAL  ENCLOSED    _______________

*SHIPPING: Orders of $15.00 or more are shipped free within the continental United States. For orders totaling less than $15.00 or those mailed to Canada or Mexico, please add $3.00 shipping. For orders shipped outside the U.S., please send $8.50 per book. Missouri residents please add 6.5% sales tax.

Name _______________________________________________________________

Address ____________________________________________________________

City ___________________________________  State _________  Zip ________

Country ____________________________________________________________

PAYMENT:
❑ Check          ❑ Money order          ❑ VISA          ❑ MasterCard

Card number: _______________________________  Exp. date:  ____ / ____

Card name: _________________________________________________________

Signature: __________________________________________________________

Please allow four to six weeks for shipping